AF616660

# Software Lifecycle Management

# The Macmillan Database/Data Communications Series

Shaku Atre, Consulting Editor

**Available**

Cave/Maymon *Software Lifecycle Management*
Fadok *Effective Design of a Codasyl Database*

**Forthcoming**

Brown/Geelen *Data Modeling in a Business Environment*
Bubley *Data Communications Systems*
Callender *An Introduction to PSL/PSA*
Cohen *A Guide to DBMs for Microcomputers*
Crout *Designing Better Systems for Endusers*
Fields *The DP/User Interface Conflict*
Ha *Digital Satellite Communications*
Musteata *How to use CICS Languages to Create On-Line Applications*
Myer *Global Communications: A Computer-Based Message System Approach*
Potter *Local Area Networks: Applications and Design*
Ranade/Ranade *VSAM: Multiprogramming with Virtual Storage*
St. Ammand *A Guide to Packet Switched Value Added Networks*
Towner *The ADS/On-Line Cookbook*

# Software Lifecycle Management:
## The Incremental Method

**William C. Cave**
*Prediction Systems, Inc.*

**Gilbert W. Maymon**
*Electronic Associates, Inc.*

Macmillan Publishing Company
*A Division of Macmillan, Inc.*
*New York*
Collier Macmillan Publishers
*London*

Macmillan Publishing Company
866 Third Avenue, New York, NY 10022

Collier Macmillan Canada, Inc.

Printed in the United States of America

printing number
1 2 3 4 5 6 7 8 9 10

**Library of Congress Cataloging in Publication Data**

Cave, William C.
Software lifecycle management.

Bibliography: p.
Includes index.
1. Computer programming management. 2. Software maintenance. I. Maymon, Gilbert W. II. Title.
III. Title: Incremental method.
QA76.6.C39 1984 001.64'2'0685 84-11264
ISBN 0-02-949210-6

*To our wives*
*Margaret Cave*
*Lois Maymon*

# Contents

# Preface

There was a time when computer programs were used primarily by the programmers who wrote them. A 16K word machine was considered very large, transistors did not exist, and neither did the term "software." Today, with the advent of timesharing and the personal computer, millions of people can use the same computer programs (software). Machines with millions of words of memory can sit on a deck like a typewriter, and their users easily can access trillions of additional words of data over standard telephone lines. The transistor as a separate circuit element has come and gone, replaced by whole computer processors. One wonders if the field of software will move as fast as that of computer hardware.

The driving force behind the rapidly moving field of computer hardware today is simply economics. It is a highly competitive environment, one in which the survivors give the customer the best price for a desired amount of computing power, in a form that is "user friendly." In fact, user friendliness is fast becoming the most important requirement in the computer field—and this is where software can take on the growth pattern of hardware.

Just as semiconductor companies make greater profits in producing products that are directly useful in a broad market, so can software companies. However, this requires the realization that the end-user environment is significantly different from the development environment. Judgments on what the end user really wants must be made in close concert with those who represent the market. Users will expect to receive a product they can easily use directly, without help or a significant learning process.

To cut the costs of supporting such a market, developers must be able to deliver systems from a distance, through standard distribution channels, without much (if any) direct contact with the customer. This requires that the software product be of high quality, both from a user and support standpoint. The software features must be easily understandable and available—on a user-friendly basis. The software must be designed to be readily supported and, in particular, easily enhanced with new features and functions. A good piece of software has a life expectancy of 15 to 20 years. It never dies. It just grows and grows!

The *incremental method* represents a pragmatic approach to managing the development and support of user-oriented software products over their lifecycles. It represents an attempt to organize and integrate a number of concepts and techniques that have evolved in the successful development of a number of large software products. We are presenting no new material. To the contrary, we have tried to sift out and use only those methods that have proved successful as gauged within a competitive software vendor environment. Unproven approaches do not fit this context. They typically carry a great risk of failure and should be avoided in a production environment. And that is what this book is about. It is aimed at helping software product managers to maximize their return on investment in software assets, while keeping risk at an acceptable level.

# Software Lifecycle Management

# CHAPTER 1

# Gaining Management Perspective

## 1.1 THE INCREMENTAL METHOD

When people invest money in stocks, mutual funds, and money markets, return on investment (ROI) is scrutinized carefully. Managers of such funds try to ensure a high probability for returning good profits along with capital. This same measure of success underlies large construction projects, including investments in new plants and new equipment. Because most people are willing to take greater risks with other people's money, income for contractors and managers of such projects must be based on performance, thereby reducing the purchaser's risk. *When tomorrow's budgets depend on today's project successes or failures, great heed must be paid to the size of risks incurred.*

Software companies that build and sell packaged products must carefully scrutinize the probability that profits will be returned on their investments. Management must carefully assess the risk of converting capital assets (which are usually scarce) into software assets that do not generate a profit. Herein lies the problem. The complexity of software, its intangible nature, and the fact that it helps implement user policy makes measuring and controlling the risk very difficult.

The *incremental method* of risk management provides a framework for partitioning software projects into "risk increments," with resources committed on a correspondingly incremental basis. The size of each increment is determined by two considerations:

- The size of each resource commitment must be commensurate with the degree of risk associated with the work to be done.
- When resources are expended and the work increment completed, the risk of project failure must have been lowered accordingly.

Risk can be quantified by defining it as the probability of *not* reaching a point where revenues (or savings) will exceed expenditures; it can be defined as the probability of exceeding budgets to the extent that the project is considered a failure; or it can be defined as the probability of having management consider the project a failure.

The incremental method responds to the observation that certain software developers have been consistently more successful than others. As used here, "success" is the delivery of a quality product, on time and within budget, that results in a high degree of *user satisfaction*. The key parameter for measuring project success is obviously user satisfaction, but when user requirements force cost estimates to exceed budget constraints, it may be necessary to relax either user requirements or budget constraints, or to halt the project. In any case, *the decision to continue a project under uncertain terms places the responsibility for failure on management.* It is essential that management provide step-by-step decision points at times when halting the project causes minimal loss of resources and continuity (especially if continuation can be justified at a later time).

The incremental method provides specific procedures and standards for reducing risk of project failure as resources are invested across the software lifecycle. The method applies to the development of automated systems in which software is a major component along the critical path. It is particularly applicable to systems involving a high degree of human interaction. The objective of the incremental method is to prepare managers for the opportunity to develop major software systems with an approach that will markedly increase the probability of success.

## 1.2 TYPES OF SOFTWARE PROJECTS

Software projects are generally spawned from external product-requesting sources. The request typically specifies one of two types of systems: custom systems or product systems.

### Custom Systems

A custom system is generally a one-of-a-kind software system specifically requested via a request for proposal (RFP) from a source outside the software development group. Typically, a contract to develop the system is agreed on after a competitive bidding process in which the prospective developers present proposals for solving the problem. For custom systems the developer must carefully analyze all of the requestor's requirements to ensure a reasonable profit margin and provide a clear understanding of all continuation or support obligations. A sophisticated requester usually provides such expectations in the RFP.

### Product Systems

A product system is one that will be sold many times. The requesting source for such systems is generally the developer's product research department. The company's internal-marketing or product-planning organization issues a product proposal that describes, in general terms, the new product's characteristics, its place in the company's overall product line, and its relationship to, or advantages over, competitive products. The basic purposes of the proposal are to demonstrate a need or opportunity to general management and to secure commitment of the resources necessary to develop the product. The proposal specifically contains the following information.

1. A brief functional description of the proposed product in terms of customer needs satisfied
2. A general statement of the target market, the company's current position in that market, and the benefits to be derived by developing the proposed product.
3. A summary analysis of major competitors and their products currently offered, or anticipated to be offered, to the target market
4. A development strategy including resource needs and cost requirements, timing requirements for introducing the product to the market, effects on existing company product lines, pricing requirements for amortization goals, and market introduction plans

The incremental method, in this case, applies to the process of justifying and obtaining the initial funding from general management so that the developing organization can produce a problem definition and project a development plan. The company is not committing itself to a full-blown, long-range development program at this time, with all of the risks and uncertainties such a commitment entails; rather it is making a modest investment to determine the feasibility of pursuing the development. If this initial phase reveals the product to be ill advised or impractical, little has been lost, and an expensive disaster has been avoided.

Although this book generally discusses the software product lifecycle (the second type of system described), the incremental method applies equally well to custom systems.

## 1.3 A REFERENCE FRAME FOR SCOPING PROJECTS

The economics of any product lifecycle depends both on the development environment and the operational (user) environment. In the case of software, the scope of problems encountered in each environment varies considerably. Software systems vary according to numbers of field installations, types of users, previous experience of both users and developers, complexity of the system due to size (e.g., number of programs, files, and so forth), and the research and development efforts required to solve technical problems.

We need a frame of reference for scoping software projects because we want to be able to estimate as accurately as possible the size of planned projects. Furthermore, we would like to look back at past project successes or failures and be able to draw accurate conclusions regarding the decisions made and value of methods used.

The reference frame used within the incremental method classifies a project according to the following dimensions:

Quality of the software product: requirements on system functional availability, reliability, and ability to respond to problems

Support requirements: number of geographically separate installations to be supported

User orientation: numbers and different types of users expected to interact with the system

Prior history: history of prior automation experience with the particular application, and difficulties encountered

Degree of complexity: number of programs, individual program complexity, and hardware complexity

Clearly, developing a single program for use by one person is far different from developing a multifaceted system for many users expecting a high-quality product at many different installations. In addition, the software developer often must contend with the parallel problem of educating inexperienced users while the software is being specified and introduced. Well-prepared, experienced management is essential in dealing with such situations.

The quality of a software product depends on the availability of system functions required by the user and the cost of maintaining that availability. Naturally, the developer constantly tries to "predict" and "control" quality from the inception of the system lifecycle; however, *in practice the final measure of quality cannot be determined until the system is in the hands of users in operational installations.*

In a multiple-installation environment, requirements for system availability and supportability are of major importance. As the number of installations and corresponding support costs rise, reliability and support requirements multiply. The nature of the support environment amplifies the need for design quality. Add to this a competitive requirement of satisfying user needs under warranty, and the result is an environment that places the highest demands on product quality and formal management control. In the commercial software vendor environment, it is difficult to sell software products without long-term warranties. Furthermore, Japanese producers are gearing up to compete. The Ministry of International Trade and Industry (MITI) has formed a review board that issues 25-year warranties on software. This competitive arena is the principal environment addressed by this book.

## 1.4 DEFINING THE SOFTWARE LIFECYCLE CONTROL PROBLEM

To start, we consider a graphical description of the lifecycle control problem. The top curve in Figure 1.1 shows rate of expenditures (dollars per month or per year) and represents resource consumption for a software product (see Norden, 1970). Assume that the rate of revenues or savings (bottom curve) can be measured in the same way as are resources consumed (dollars per month or per year). From this one can derive a clear measure (dollars and cents) of the return on investment (ROI) that can be achieved.

Such a measure can be precisely determined for a software vendor marketing a package product. This measure is also valid for products in which savings can be clearly determined. In cases where these measures are not so clear, there appears to be little doubt that the incremental method is directly applicable, although its evaluation may be more subjective.

The curves shown in Figure 1.1 provide a graphical representation of the software lifecycle control problem. This graphical representation is a general one because, for a given software problem, there can be an infinite set of possible curves. The curve's actual shape depends on judgments of the project manager as well as on many other factors across the lifecycle. The technical problem objective is to shape these curves in such a way as to maximize ROI.

Managers of large software projects must face many external con-

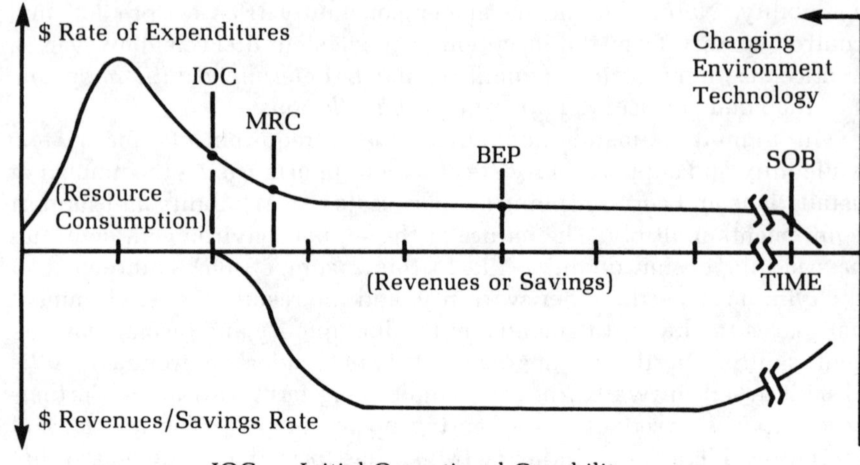


**Figure 1.1.** The Software System Lifecycle.

straints. First, managers must determine the time period during which a market for the product is expected. In other words, they must determine the period during which revenues for the system will flow or savings will accrue. They must consider the changing environment, changing technology, competition, and the fact that at some time in the future the technology or market requirement will become obsolete.

If a market already exists for the system, the start of revenues, or initial operational capability (IOC), will depend only on development time to achieve the goal. The period for revenues is bound by IOC and system obsolescence (SOB). Obviously, if more money is spent up front to shorten the time to IOC, revenues will begin to come in earlier. However, the experienced project manager is aware that there is no even dollar-for-dollar tradeoff, and, in fact, the cost to do things faster can rise exponentially.

Other external financial constraints that must be considered are maximum resource consumption (MRC) and break-even point (BEP). MRC occurs when current (for example, monthly) revenues or savings exceed current expenses. Enough financial resources must be available at the rate required to cover those utilized to MRC. If this point is not estimated properly and, consequently, never reached, the project can terminate because of lack of funds. BEP occurs when total expenses have been recovered via revenues or savings. Vendor profits cannot be realized until this point, except through long-term capitalization of the up-front peak costs. In any event, a vendor facing many years to BEP, will be considering other places to invest resources.

In summary, the software lifecycle control problem is reduced to one of shaping the curves in Figure 1.1 in such a way that maximizes ROI while meeting constraints on factors such as quality, risk, MRC, time to IOC, and BEP.

In their paper, "Bankruptcy of Software Projects," Abe and coauthors (1979) report a number of software projects in which the lifecycle consumption function took on the "double hump" form of Figure 1.2. The major observable characteristic of such projects was that as operational testing got underway, working toward IOC, it became apparent that the software product did not exist to the degree imagined by the project management. Simply stated, management thought the product was ready for delivery when, in fact, it was not. This situation usually is not discovered until operational testing is well underway, a common software dilemma. Interpreted another way, the risk of project failure remained high as the project approached it's "planned" IOC. Figure 1.2 shows a fairly typical example of a poorly managed project.

Figure 1.3 shows the desired risk-reduction curve characteristic of a well-managed project. Risk of failure should be relatively low as the project approaches its planned IOC. To achieve this degree of control, the following must be true:

- Risk must be measurable from the beginning of the lifecycle. That is, we must be able to *audit the state of the software* at key points along the lifecycle to determine the level of risk at those points.
- Risk must be controllable to the extent that, given we can complete a

**Figure 1.2.** A Poorly Managed Project.

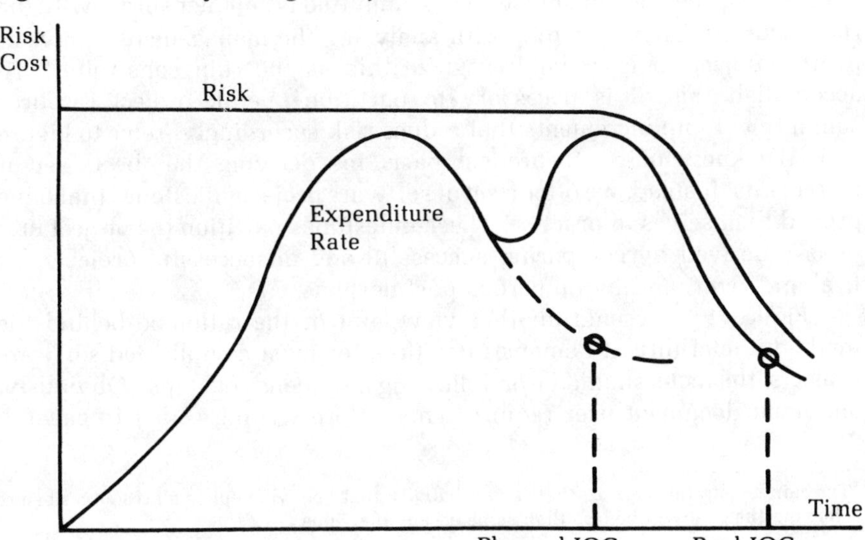

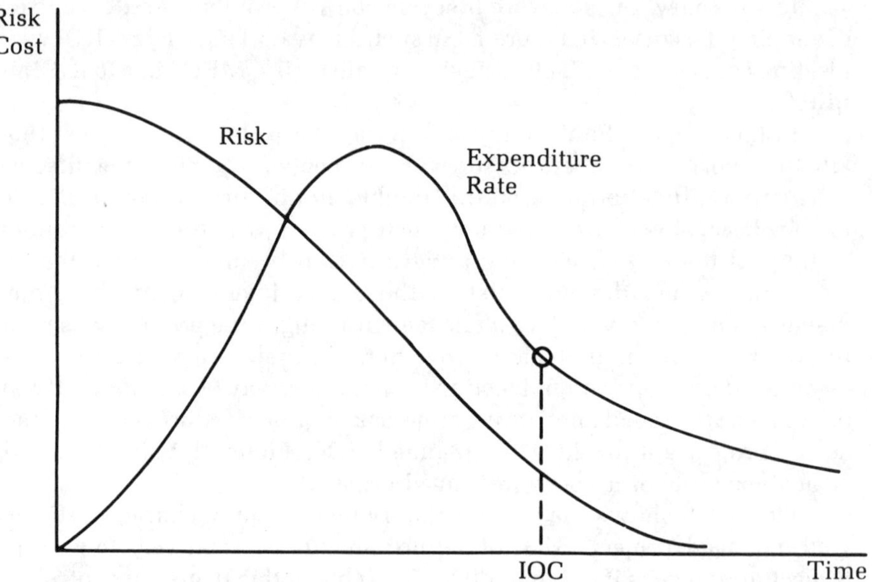


**Figure 1.3.** A Well-Managed Project.

specific set of tasks toward building the final product, we can then *accurately project the reduction in risk* achieved by completing those tasks.

Let us translate these basic concepts into practical management methods.

The underlying theme of the incremental method is to invest resources (make resource commitments) across the project lifecycle in a way that ensures that the portion of resources committed is commensurate with the risk incurred. Those familiar with analyzing the management of investments subject to loss will recognize this as the ruin constraint.* To accomplish this, it is necessary to partition overall project resource commitment into increments that reduce risk accordingly (refer to Figure 1.4). We know of no theoretical basis for deriving the "best" set of increments. Instead, we offer a set of software project milestones that have proved themselves in practice. These milestones partition the project into phases derived by comparing successful and unsuccessful projects, by trial and error, and by numerous postmortems.

Figure 1.5 presents another viewpoint of the rationale behind the method. Pictorially, it demonstrates that, for most complicated software projects, the focus should be on following a sequence of steps. (Obviously, one must document user requirements before writing code.) In general,

*The ruin constraint requires that the probability that one will deplete all resources before achieving the goal will be less than some acceptable value.

concurrent developments of major system functions rely on the validity of "parallel" assumptions, and such parallel assumptions have been the cause of many project failures.

Figure 1.6 shows a less risky approach. Although this sequential approach may not appeal to anyone who is in a hurry, the following points justify its use.

- Reflection on successful projects where this approach was used indicates substantially more time would have been lost on many potential "parallel" opportunities had they been taken.
- Postmortems on unsuccessful projects clearly demonstrate that a sequential process would have avoided decisions to continue to meet self-imposed deadlines that were unrealistic.
- Decisions to terminate projects, with the possibility of restarting later, would have come more easily.

It is this sequential milestone approach that provides the basis for the incremental method.

**Figure 1.4.** Partitioning the Lifecycle into Risk Increments.

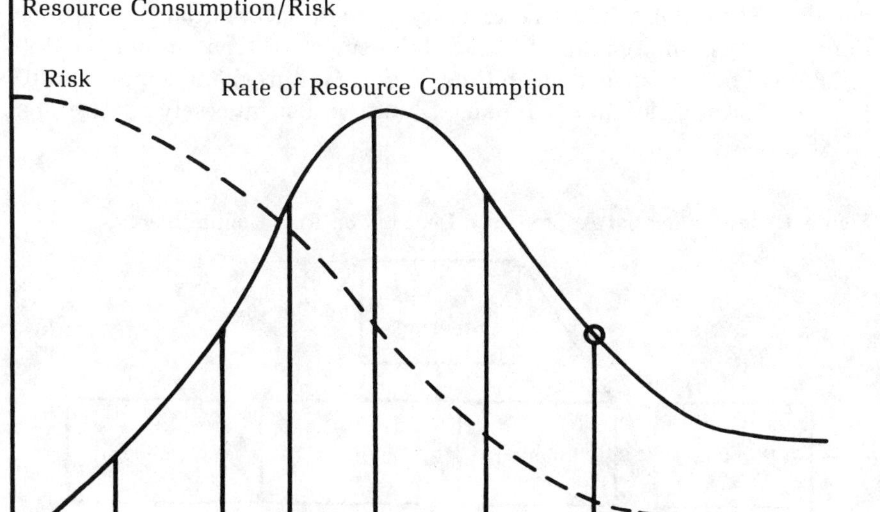

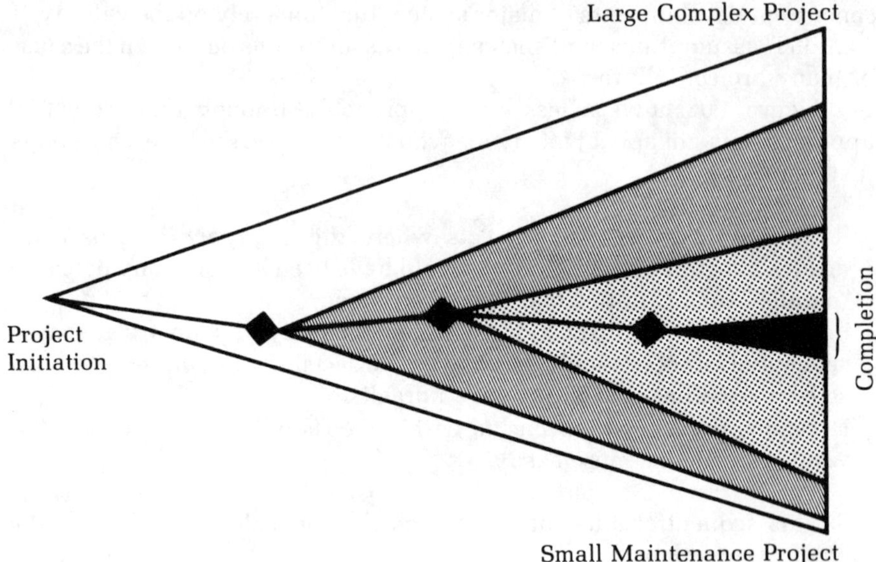


**Figure 1.5.** Focusing on a Valid Solution Range in a Sequence of Steps.

## 1.5 DETERMINING SOFTWARE QUALITY

Various measures of software quality have been offered in the literature (Cave and Salisbury, 1978; Wilbur, 1981). The one used here is described in detail in Section 8.3. Intuitively, it says that software quality is proportional to system availability. Availability is in turn proportional to reliability (in the sense of mean time between failures) and supportability (in the sense of mean time to repair). Quality is also inversely proportional

**Figure 1.6.** A Sequential Approach to Decision on Risk Commitments.

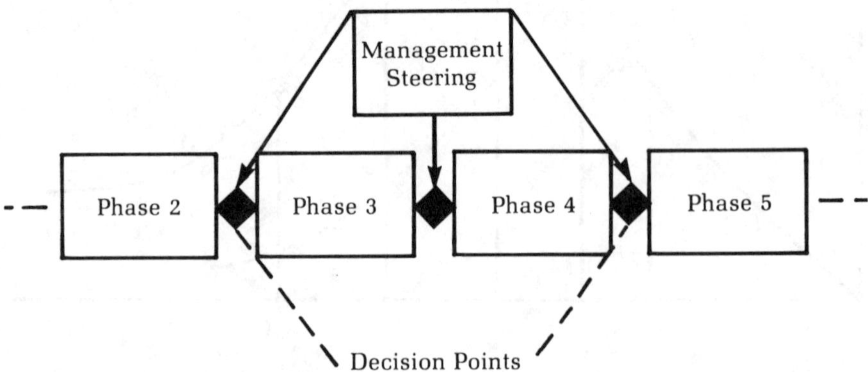

to the costs of maintaining the availability. Quality as here defined can only be measured after IOC, in a live user environment. Before IOC, software quality can be predicted and controlled by measuring factors that affect it; however, the measure of quality in a live user environment is considered essential in validating the effects of such factors.

In the commercial vendor environment, prospective buyers of a software system will want to talk with existing users about the availability of desired system functions because this is the quality of the product as seen by the user. This aspect is only part of the picture as seen by a vendor supporting a system under warranty. From the vendor's perspective, the cost of support in determining ROI must be considered. To be a high-quality product, the software system must be inexpensive to support.

To build a high-quality product, the vendor must invest more time and money during development, before IOC. It is left to the project manager to determine an adequate level of availability, below which the risk of losing anticipated revenues or savings becomes too high. Project management judgment of such an acceptable level of quality certainly will depend much more on user needs and the capability of the competition than on numbers one might obtain from equations such as derived in Section 8.3. However, the prudent software developer will not disregard such measures because as users become more sophisticated, quantitative measures will become more important.

## 1.6 MEASURING SUCCESS IN A COMPETITIVE ENVIRONMENT

Having defined the software lifecycle control problem, we now consider how the project manager can achieve practical solutions. Questions to be answered are: What controls shape the curves in Figure 1.1? How can we predict their responses? How can we validate our predictions in a changing environment? We approach these questions by comparing vendors of software products in a competitive environment (see Figure 1.7). Before we examine specific case studies, let's look at some general conclusions drawn from observation.

1. Certain software developers have been consistently more successful than others.
2. It is commonly thought that risk can be reduced by going slowly, particularly if management is inexperienced; however, going slowly may not minimize risk in the way we defined earlier and, in fact, can decrease ROI dramatically.
3. The steep rate of resource utilization by Developer 1 (Figure 1.7) requires a knowledge of how to use those resources effectively—in other words, management experience that supports good judgment.

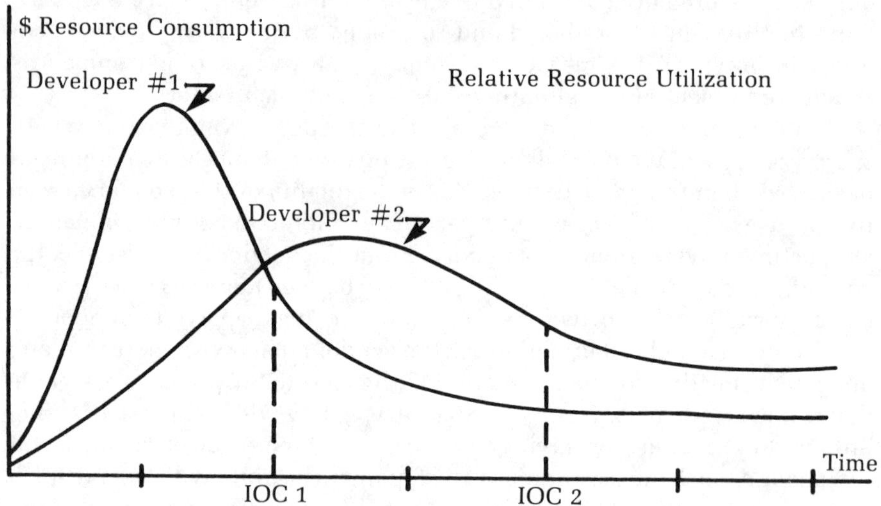


**Figure 1.7.** Comparison of the Resource Consumption Rates of Different Software Developers.

4. It is important to understand how and where software fits into the lifecycle of total systems and to what degree software lifecycle management influences total system management.

Software is different from hardware. Probably the most significant difference is the shape of the resource utilization curve across the lifecycle. Figure 1.8 indicates the consumption of resources across the lifecycle for typical hardware system. Note that the peak occurs well after IOC. In typical software lifecycles that have been characterized by Norden (1970) and Putnam (1976), the peak occurs substantially before IOC. When software consumes a major portion of the system lifecycle resources, it is necessary to get top management understanding and approval of early peak resource utilization. If this is not done and one attempts to meet the same IOC, that IOC will be premature. This results in a fictitious operational capability wherein the user is led to believe that a real operational capability exists. Continuing software development while under live operation can cause trauma in the marketplace unless such development was specifically planned.

In addition to software resource consumption being different from that of hardware, the software lifecycle has a different set of natural intrinsic milestones. Unless these are mapped properly into the total system lifecycle and made clearly visible, the software part of the system will not be properly controlled. The typical set of hardware system lifecycle milestones and activities can be used for software without much

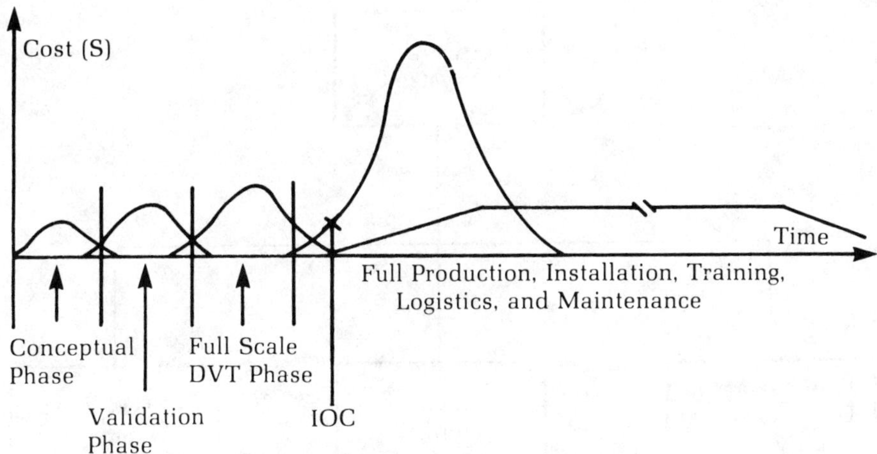


**Figure 1.8.** A Typical Hardware Lifecycle Consumption Function.

change in terms of names and general achievement. What is required is proper interpretation and a different set of specific measurement criteria for milestone attainment. This requirement for management milestones and standards peculiar to software is most important to recognize.

## 1.7 STRUCTURE AND DEFINITION OF THE SOFTWARE PRODUCT

In the competitive product vendor environment, one is forced to find ways to cut costs while achieving high quality. Under the strain of good competition, vendors find ways to do both. The first step is to organize in a way that provides the measurement and control that a project manager needs. An often overlooked framework is a clear definition of the software end product.

The software product generally consists of three libraries: the external documentation library, the program library, and the test library (see Figure 1.9). Of these three the most important is the external documentation library shown in Figures 1.10 and 1.11. In a well-disciplined development environment, the external documentation is completed before programming. Any coding done before completion of this library is for validation of approach, not for production. This discipline forces an orderly approach to the system design process, which is embodied in the development of the external documentation in increasing layers of detail. The program library (Figure 1.12) and the test library (Figure 1.13) can be developed concurrently once the external documentation library is complete. The formality and discipline used to develop and maintain these

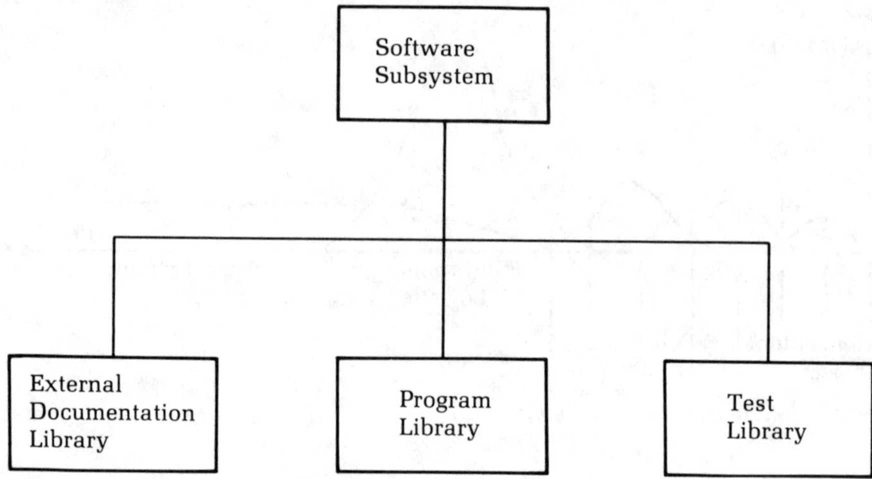


**Figure 1.9.** The Software End-Product.

libraries will impart a major influence on their quality and, therefore, the quality of the software end product.

## 1.8 A TYPICAL PRODUCT CASE HISTORY

Product quality as described in the previous sections can and must be designed and built into a system from its inception. This can only be achieved through a formal management discipline that must be introduced at many points throughout the system lifecycle. The ease with which such a discipline can be invoked and enforced depends on the understanding, perspective, and experience of all contributors to the project. It also depends on the means for practical enforcement. A project manager must have some key members of his technical staff who understand the need for discipline, and must be provided with an environment for enforcement.

The requirement for a formal discipline exists at interfaces between the system manager and other elements involved in the system lifecycle as indicated in Figure 1.14. To facilitate understanding of the discipline required at these interfaces, consider the following typical vendor predicament. A system has moved to the installation and support phase of its lifecycle, with installation under way at the seventh user location. Three users are calling for a software change that they claim will provide a substantial reduction in personnel skills required at an important human interface. This change appears trivial to the users but will ripple through a major part of the system. Of the potential user market it is determined that

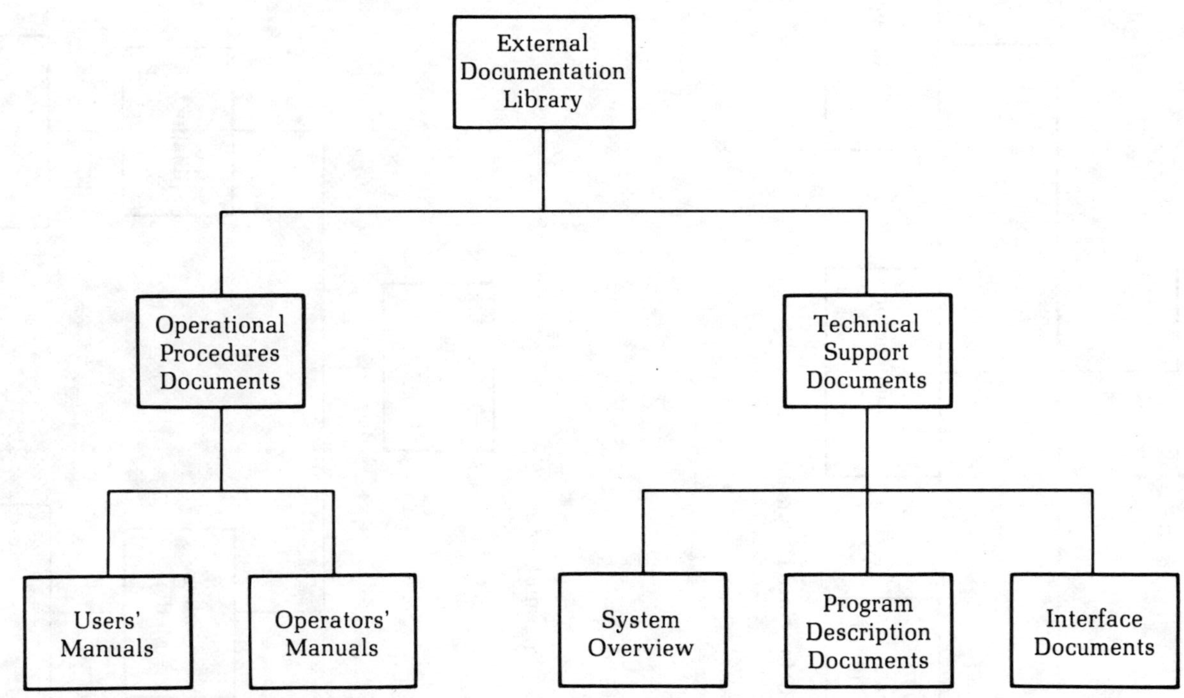


**Figure 1.10.** External Documentation Library.

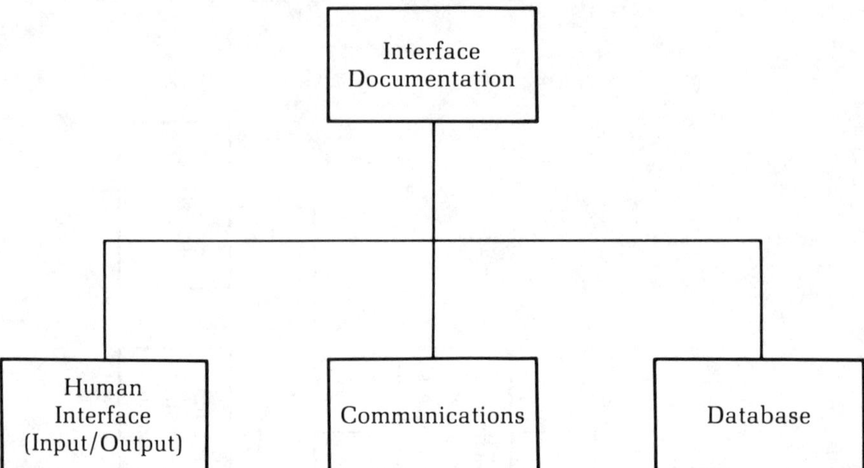


**Figure 1.11.** Interface Documentation.

**Figure 1.12.** Program Library.

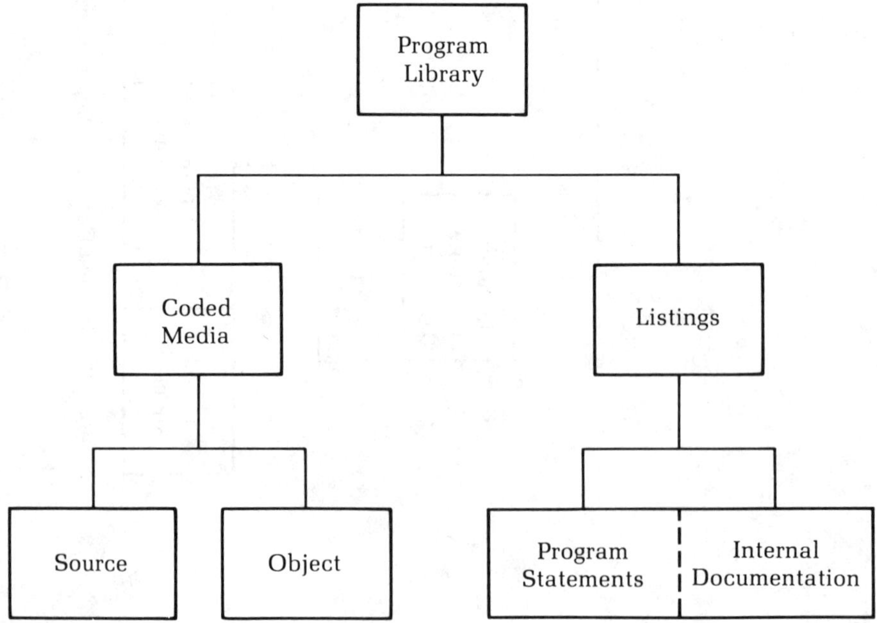

35% will want the change, and prospective buyers are talking to existing users as well as to competitors. Finally, marketing is encouraging the technical support group to make a "quick fix" at their showplace installation as a way of proving to prospects that the change is in.

In the vendor environment described, it is important that decisions on such quick fix changes be made on a sound economic basis. If a decision is made to implement such a change, it must be done under tight control, or system quality can be badly degraded and future market losses incurred. Before giving birth to a new version of the system, management must consider the following:

1. Can a single system identity be preserved, or will maintaining separate versions for different market segments be necessary, and at what cost?
2. What will the costs be for design, documentation, development, and formal testing?
3. What will the cost be for upgrading all existing installations if a unique identity is to be preserved?
4. How will testing, training, and maintenance procedures be affected and at what cost?

The quality of the total system product will weigh heavily in the ongoing costs of installation, training, and maintenance, particularly if software implements user policies and procedures.

**Figure 1.13.** Test Library.

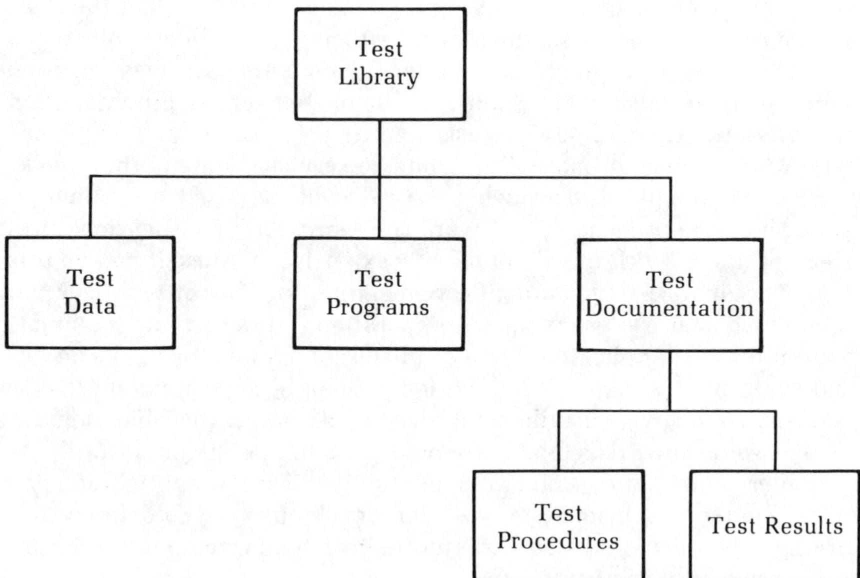

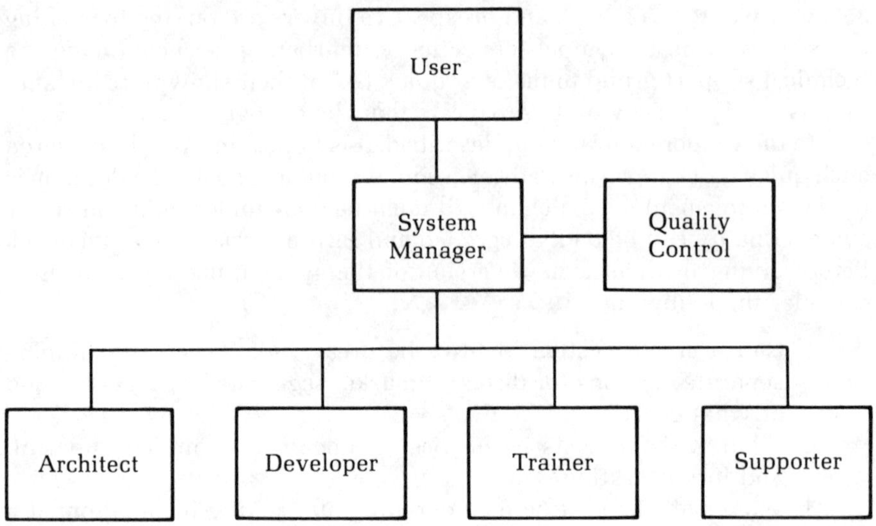


**Figure 1.14.** Formal System Manager Interfaces.

## 1.9 A CUSTOM SYSTEM CONTRACT CASE HISTORY

Before we describe the methods contained in the latter sections of this book, it is important to present the context of requirements imposed within a custom system contract environment. Using a representative case history, we start at the beginning—reviewing the user's predicament. User top management, headed by a strong president, believed that the sea of paperwork and miscalculations within their corporation could not be overcome except through automation. This situation was of prime importance because it presented a major barrier to growth, which otherwise was inevitable. The user had no prior automation experience except for a minor brush with an outside service company that quickly terminated in failure. Through personal contact based on reputation, management appraoched a software company. After a brief look at the user's problem (with the aid of outside expertise, because it had no prior experience in the particular application of interest), the software company determined that the user's mode of operation did not fit into a standard pattern for that application because of special manufacturing techniques that could not be changed. In addition, it soon became apparent that the user's personnel were hostile to the idea of automating their functions. If a system were to be developed, it would have to operate on a third-party computer center. This center was close to the user but approximately 30 miles from the developer. Access for development would have to be strictly scheduled, and there was no room for nonproduction (development) oriented work facilities.

The end result was that the developer bid competitively and made a profit, and the user happily tripled sales volume and profits during the first year after the system was installed.

We highlight the following requirements based on observation:

1. It was necessary to break the project into manageable pieces (phases) allowing for maximum control on the part of both user and developer. *These phases were funded incrementally.*
2. It was necessary to allow for well-controlled changes in user requirements.
3. It was necessary to allow for review, justification, and a go–no go decision to preceed with a modified plan after each phase.
4. It was necessary to allow for gaps between phases because of scheduling of management reviews, the incorporation of design changes, and staffing for the next phase.
5. It was necessary to allow time for the developer to gain experience as well as discover the peculiarities and exceptions within the given application.
6. It was necessary to allow time to expose the user's personnel to relevant computer techniques.
7. It was necessary to implement a highly structured set of rules and standards with practical means of review and enforcement.

The successful accommodation of these requirements was accomplished using the *management plan* and *standards* described within the incremental method.

# CHAPTER 2

# The Incremental Method

## 2.1 ELEMENTS ESSENTIAL TO SUCCESS

The incremental method is based on the premise that three elements are essential to the success of any system development. These elements are: experienced management, a conducive work environment, and good methods and supporting tools to execute the work. The basic concepts underlying these essential elements are offered in the following sections.

### Management

*The development of user-oriented software systems is first and foremost a management problem.* It may be difficult for management to accept this premise because poor management reflects to the top of any organization. Nevertheless, this premise is essential inasmuch as project failures generally result from poor judgment by inexperienced management, not a lack of technical ability. The recognition of this premise is required to bring about successful development of a highly user-oriented software system.

These conclusions have been drawn from the following observations. First, the responsibility for implementing policy and managerial procedures to be used in final operational systems is implicitly given to the software developer. The reason, which is not readily apparent, is that the very nature of software development—creating a decision process—places this responsibility on those doing the creating. Second, it is apparent that good knowledge, experience, and judgment are most effective when provided with sufficient perspective. Without this perspective, decisions to reduce risk, avoid major mistakes in policy, and affect successful direction cannot be made. This concept is underscored by the following:

- The importance of gathering knowledge and weighing judgments regarding the experience, skills, and tools required to complete a given task in a highly structured environment
- The deliberate comparison of those requirements to the existing as well as unavailable resources within the organization
- The importance of seeking out and learning from another's experience, even a competitor
- Recognition of the need to contract for special expertise and the importance of establishing the credibility of outside experts through reliable references
- The importance of maintaining constant vigilance against sacrificing effectiveness for efficiency, or engaging the concurrent development of dependent efforts

### Environment

The success of an organization whose responsibility is the development of user-oriented systems is finally measured by the willingness on the part of prospective users to order and pay for services rendered on a long-term, continuing basis. An essential element among those organizations with outstanding long-term profit records is the creation of an environment that emphasizes responsiveness to user requirements and their satisfaction—on time and within budget. When dollar control flows directly from the end user down through the ranks of the developer, management ability is more clearly measured by the bottom line. The resulting environment is less prone to politics, convoluted technical approaches, and intelligence demonstrations. Such an environment creates a willingness to call on outside expertise, eliminating the not-invented-here (NIH) factor. It creates a need for accurate performance measurement, as well as a steering capability through management emphasis so that response to direction can be achieved.

In summary, software development requires a highly structured work environment, similar to that of a large construction project. *Without an environment that affords proper control and response, the most capable managers will be stifled.*

### Methodology

There is no simple methodology for developing a large construction project. This fact is apparent from the visibility of different project phases and the obvious separation of tasks to be performed. For similar reasons, although not so obvious, there is no simple technique for developing the types of software systems investigated here. In practice, a set of *management guidelines* on the utilization of a *plan* for acquiring and maintaining project control has been used successfully. In addition, this plan must be backed by a set of *standards*, without which control cannot be maintained.

The incremental method of risk management can be viewed as a general plan for the development of large, user-oriented software systems (Figure 2.1). Acceptance of such a plan *establishes* good management control at the outset of a project. In addition, good management control is best *maintained* through the use of a set of standards that supports the entire lifecycle. A set of integrated standards is provided to accomplish this. These standards are "integrated" in the sense that they all relate directly to the general plan put forth in the incremental method.

## 2.2 ESTABLISHING CONTROL

### Lifecycle Planning

Successful lifecycle planning must provide for an incremental commitment of resources. As described in Chapter 1, increment size can be determined by the time frame and resources required to achieve a measurable milestone and the risk of not achiving that milestone. A set of milestones based on those used successfully in the past by various software developers is offered in the following paragraphs. These milestones segment the software development cycle into sequential phases. Each phase should be terminated with thorough documentation of work completed, a critical review, a detailed plan for the next phase, and an updated overall plan for the remainder of the project. A go-no go decision can then be made regarding commitment of resources for the next phase, and changes resulting from review are formally incorporated into any continuation plan, and the next phase is initiated.

### Risk Increments and Management Milestones

Following is a set of management milestones for controlling software life cycles:

1. *Project definition.* The problem must be defined in general terms. Basic user objectives and constraints must be agreed on, along with an

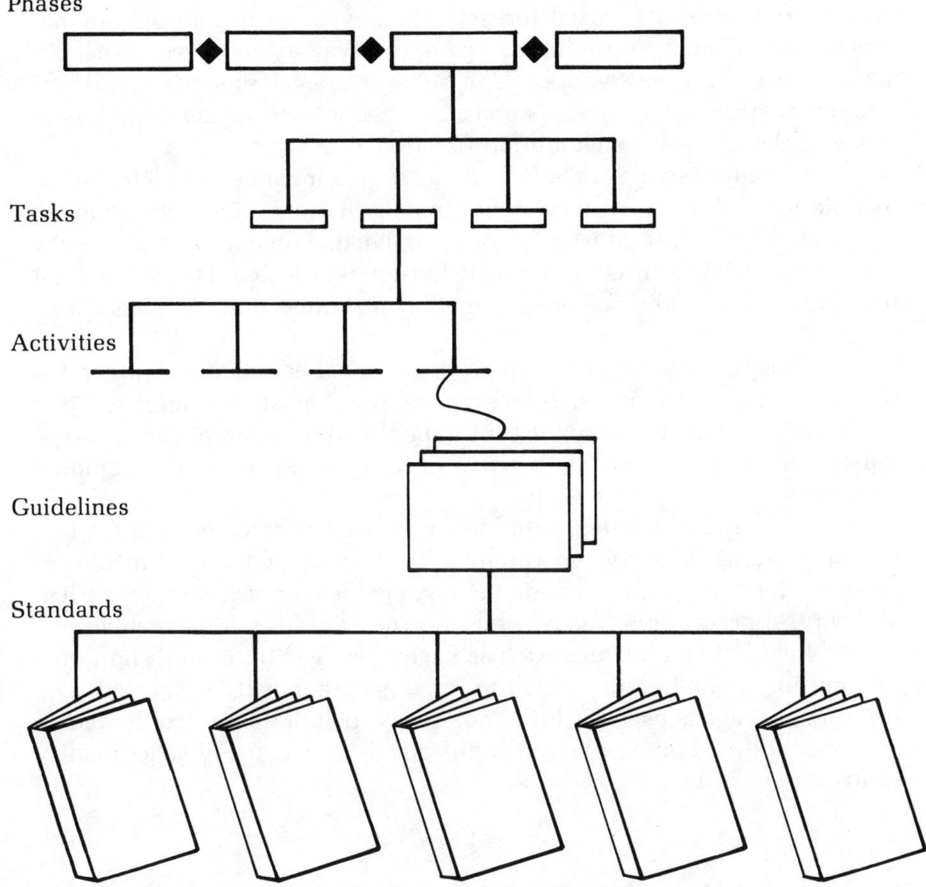


**Figure 2.1.** Structure of the Management Guidelines and Standards.

overall plan and gross estimate of resources required. This plan must include sufficient resource commitments from the user or user representatives to participate in the effort required to completely specify the detailed functional and performance requirements of the system.

2. *Functional analysis and specification.* User requirements must be analyzed, and detailed functional specifications must be developed for the system and expressed in a manner that is easily understood by the end user. Mock-up demonstrations may be required, using terminal equipments and throw-away software to simulate man-machine or intersystem interfaces. Proper completion of this milestone depends heavily on the user's commitment of resources to the task.

3. *Environment analysis and specification.* Implementation and development requirements, such as equipment configuration, languages, and support software to be used for both the development and operational environments, must be produced. Again, throwaway software for benchmark testing may be required. The software development/support environment specified during this phase is a major factor in determining the shape of the lifecycle consumption function.

4. *System design.* A detailed system design must be completed to the module level. A detailed documentation set and a detailed development and testing schedule must also be completed. Substantial throwaway software may be required to complete the detailed design. The documentation and test plans and procedures are the most important products of this phase.

5. *Program development.* All programs must be coded and integrated into a working system. A regression test set must be completed and available for quality control of future modifications. A training package must also be completed. The system is fully tested in the development environment.

6. *Operational testing.* Initial users utilize the complete system in a carefully maintained, live operational environment. Quality control procedures, (for example, regression testing, independent acceptance testing, and control procedures covering all libraries) are fully implemented.

7. *Installation and support.* The system is distributed and supported for multiple installations, which may be geographically separated. The training package is used for bringing up new installations. The system is corrected, refined, and enhanced until obsolescence, using strict quality control procedures.

## Establishing a Proper Management Environment

Software lifecycle project control must be established with the acceptance of a formal management plan based on measurable milestones such as those just offered. This formal management plan must contain realistic estimates of time and resources required across the system lifecycle. However, accurate estimates cannot be expected to be derived during the initial phase of the project. Therefore, it is essential that both the user and the developer's top management understand the incremental approach, which is based on minimizing the risk of wasting resources.

In a highly competitive vendor environment, decisions to terminate work on potential product line systems are not uncommon in view of changing market emphasis and technology. If each phase is properly documented at its termination point, projects can be shelved for periods and then restarted at the next phase with minimal loss of continuity.

Although one may believe that the level of documentation can be lessened to some degree to minimize time delays for urgently needed systems, documentation should never be eliminated in the name of expediency. The best solution in such a case is to apply additional resources to achieve the required schedule while ensuring adequate quality of the end product.

Managers must be constantly reminded that the decision to continue a project under uncertain terms places the responsibility for failure on them. Major decisions should be based only on well-documented facts. This formality puts performance measurement and enforcement of discipline on a practical basis. Practical enforcement ultimately lies with management review of the written record! Unless a clear set of specifications, documentation, and plans for the next phase are formally written, reviewed, and approved, the next phase should not be started.

## 2.3 MAINTAINING CONTROL

A good management plan is essential to establishing project control. Equally important are good management policies, procedures, and standards for maintaining project control and, particularly, continual control over quality of the software product.

### Measuring Milestone Achievement

An integrated set of software development standards is the best measure of milestone achievement. Because operating environments and physical facilities can vary widely, we have not attempted to introduce an operating standard; however, because the development and support environments are crucial, we have addressed them Chapter 10. The integrated set of standards used to support the incremental method are highlighted in the following paragraphs:

1. *Project definition standard.* This standard is necessary as a guide to defining and planning projects *in writing* during the initial phase. It provides the guidelines for problem definition in management-oriented terms; it also provides guidelines for writing an initial project plan. These standards are discussed in Chapter 4.

2. *Functional analysis/specification standard.* The period for analysis and specification of functional requirements should be used to demonstrate the organization, expertise, and credibility of the developer in the eyes of the user. The results offer viable project success or coin failure. In Chapter 5, standards are offered as a written collection of experience in performing what in some cases is an awesome task.

3. *Documentation standard.* Fortunately, much work has been done to set standards for documenting a large software system. The critical nature of the documentation process in large user-oriented software projects has led to the standard outlined here. The differences between the proposed standard and those we have reviewed are sufficiently great to warrant the sample. In particular, the following major differences exist:

*Integrated approach:* Various existing documentation standards create the need for an integrated approach to project planning and standards. In fact, many documentation manuals tell how to plan the development effort, obviating the need for what is proposed here.

*Top down design:* Experience indicates that the most practical implementation and enforcement of "top down" design, as described by Baker (1972), is through continual refinement of the documentation set. The documentation standards must accommodate this design process.

Two other items are worthy of attention. First, within a documentation standard it is important to tell *when* as well as *how*. The standard presented here provides a time schedule that relates to the time phase plan of the incremental method. Second, the importance of controlling the integrity and distribution of a large documentation library cannot be overemphasized. Documentation standards are discussed in Chapter 6.

4. *Programming standard.* Although many programming standards exist today, they are not publicized for at least two reasons: first, a programming standard is highly language-dependent, requiring that separate standards be written for each language; second, programming standards have been highly stylized, and therefore they depend on individual preferences. Recent concepts, in particular those developed by Mills (1972), provide a sound basis for standardized style and structure. It is anticipated that these concepts will promote the use of programming standards on a widespread basis, at least for the more popular languages. The general requirements for programming standards are provided elsewhere (see, for example, Spier, 1974). Programming standards are discussed in Chapter 7.

5. *Testing and quality control standard.* Standards for testing and quality control appear to be common only to those organizations developing large-scale systems. Not much material is publicly available. Certainly, Sherr's paper (1972) is a major contribution on system testing and integration. One observes the analogy to a large construction project with major emphasis on a sensible construction schedule. Improved scheduling can be obtained through the use of stubbing techniques, as defined by Baker (1972); however, their implementation is more difficult when programs are not broken down into a treelike structure. The requirements

for quality control are well described by Bloom and coauthors (1973). Good support software and library facilities are essential. Standards to support testing and quality control are discussed in Chapter 8.

### Predicting and Tracking Progress

There is no substitute for good judgment and experience in estimating the time and resources required for software development; however, practical quantitative methods are available for aiding the project manager in this task. Norden (1970) has characterized the software lifecycle resource consumption function. Putnam (1976) has extended this work to estimate time and resource requirements via regression analysis. A comparison of techniques for cost estimating is provided in Chapter 4, Section 4.4.

Putnam's method appears to be directly applicable to prediction of the consumption function based on the previously described milestones in the following way. If, instead of using the slope of the function at a particular point of time, one were to use the area under the curve as the time required to complete initial phases of the lifecycle, it should be possible to apply similar regression analysis to determine areas required for future phases. This process is discussed in more detail in Chapter 4.

Probably the best way to track progress is by rate charting, as described by Snyder (1976). Rate charting has the distinct advantage of allowing the project manager to track the rate of change of progress, in addition to status. Such tracking provides an excellent means for flagging activities that are falling behind. Rate charting is a practical method for preventing a crisis management situation.

### Controlling System Quality

"Software quality control has been a major contributing factor in producing and sustaining the high reliability and quality of software in the Bell System's Number 1 Electronic Switching System (ESS)" (Bloom et al., 1973). Control of system quality starts at the beginning of the lifecycle. The initial project plan must provide the resources necessary to ensure that the specification, documentation, program, and test libraries that make up the software product are constantly audited, not just reviewed. Formal audit procedures and reports are the only practical means of enforcing standards.

Configuration management and regression testing become most important in the deployment and support phases of the lifecycle. Unless proper configuration management controls and regression test procedures are developed, the system can easily go out of control as multiple installations go live because software, unlike hardware, requires that the product specification and design be changed every time software maintenance is performed. In addition, one uses software because of the economic advantages involved in making changes. No one would conceive of building into hardware everything that has been built into software. The costs would be too great!

### Making Decisions in a Changing Environment

The development of large software systems with long lifecycles must take into account changing requirements and technology. By breaking the resource commitment to risk increments as we have defined, project managers are afforded time to anticipate and make decisions in a changing environment.

## 2.4 BENEFITS OF THE INCREMENTAL METHOD

Structuring of the overall software development cycle into sequential phases affords the following advantages:

1. Allowance for learning experience to be gained in successive phases with particular applications so that subsequent phases can be planned more carefully and realistically
2. Allowance for review and justification to suggest a modified plan after each phase, allowing maximum management control
3. Allowance for changes in project emphasis, project time frame, project environment, and personnel assignments, with minimal loss of project coherence
4. Allowance for gaps between phases owing to personnel acquisition, hardware acquisition, and market justification/priority
5. Allowance for continual user interaction, refinement, and review of specifications and documentation on an increasingly detailed basis before each phase commits more resources.

Because the termination of each phase represents the passing of a major milestone along the path to project completion, interative decision processes, shown schematically in Figure 2.2, can be strictly maintained within phases. This approach emphasizes the importance of making the correct decisions in early phases and the need for "look ahead" to problems that might occur during later phases. This look-ahead process depends to a great extent on knowing where and for what to look.

This concept of early phase emphasis and "look ahead" is sometimes called front-end-loading. The concept must be sold to the customer when the custom system is being built because, under an incremental funding arrangement, it appears that the customer is paying a high price in the

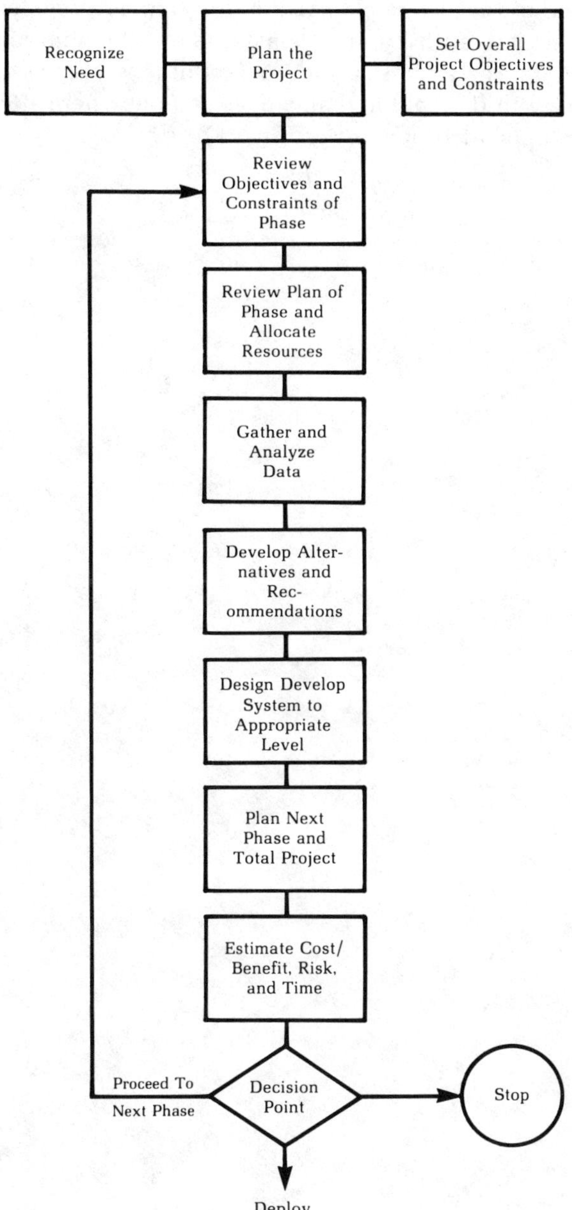


**Figure 2.2.** Decision Processes.

beginning and is getting less. When the detailed documentation is completed (end of the design phase) and program development is about to start, customers are entirely enthusiastic about the approach. Although higher during the early phases, the product of (cost) × (risk of failure) is flat compared with the bubble that can occur somewhere after the start of program development (refer to Section 1.4).

# CHAPTER 3

# The Management Plan

## 3.1 INTRODUCTION

The management plan outlined in this chapter is organized according to the phases of the incremental method. Because most of the detailed techniques are contained in other chapters, the plan appears here in skeletal form. It is intended to serve as a guide. The developer can select the appropriate techniques depending on project scope and requirements encountered. There can be no substitute for good judgment.

## 3.2 INCREMENTAL DEVELOPMENT PHASES

The flow and dependence of the tasks described for each phase are illustrated in Figure 3.1 and placed into overall perspective in Figure 3.2. The numbers within the circles represent the respective paragraph numbers of this section.

*Project Definition and Planning (Phase I)*

I-1 *Staffing*
The anticipated project leader and his or her manager should work closely to develop the documents required for completion of

**Figure 3.1.** Incremental Management Plan.

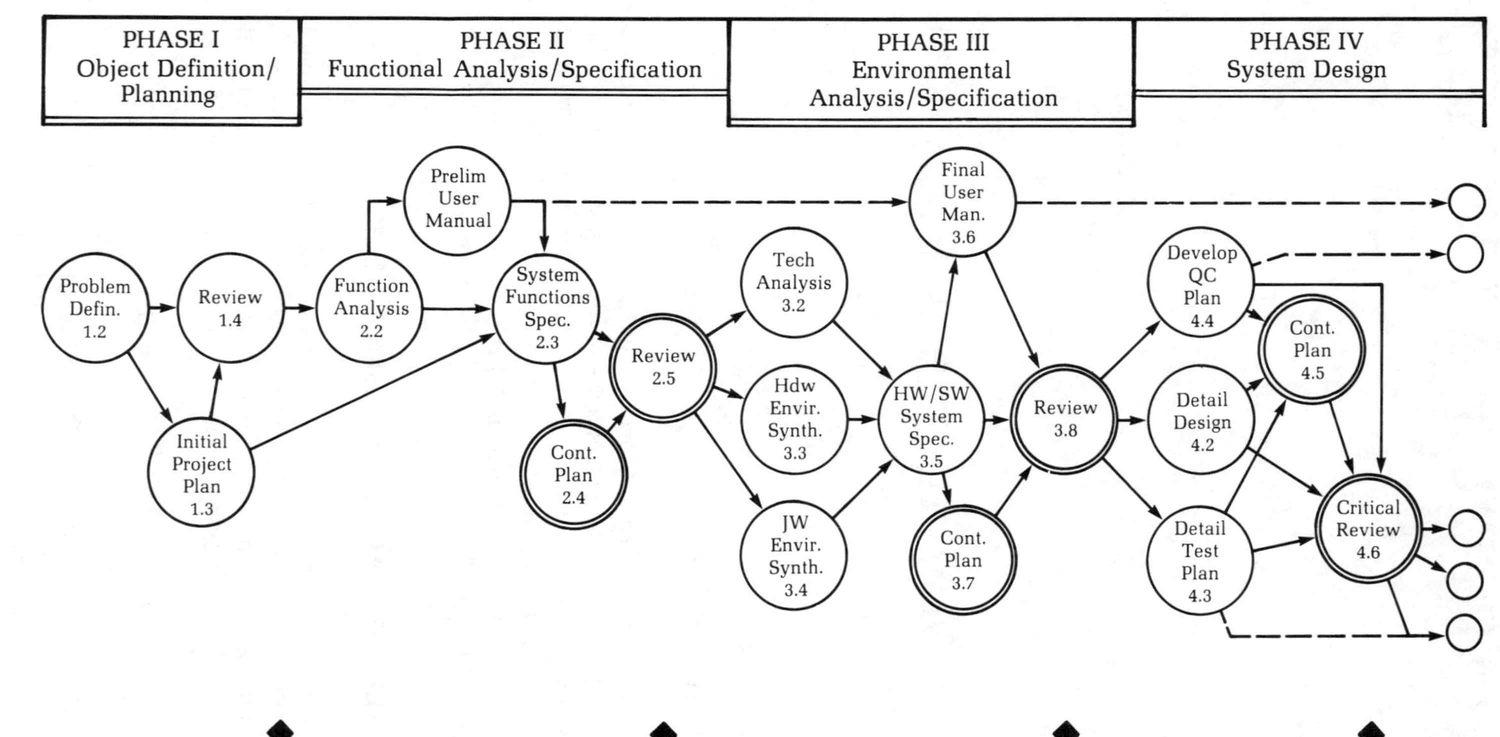

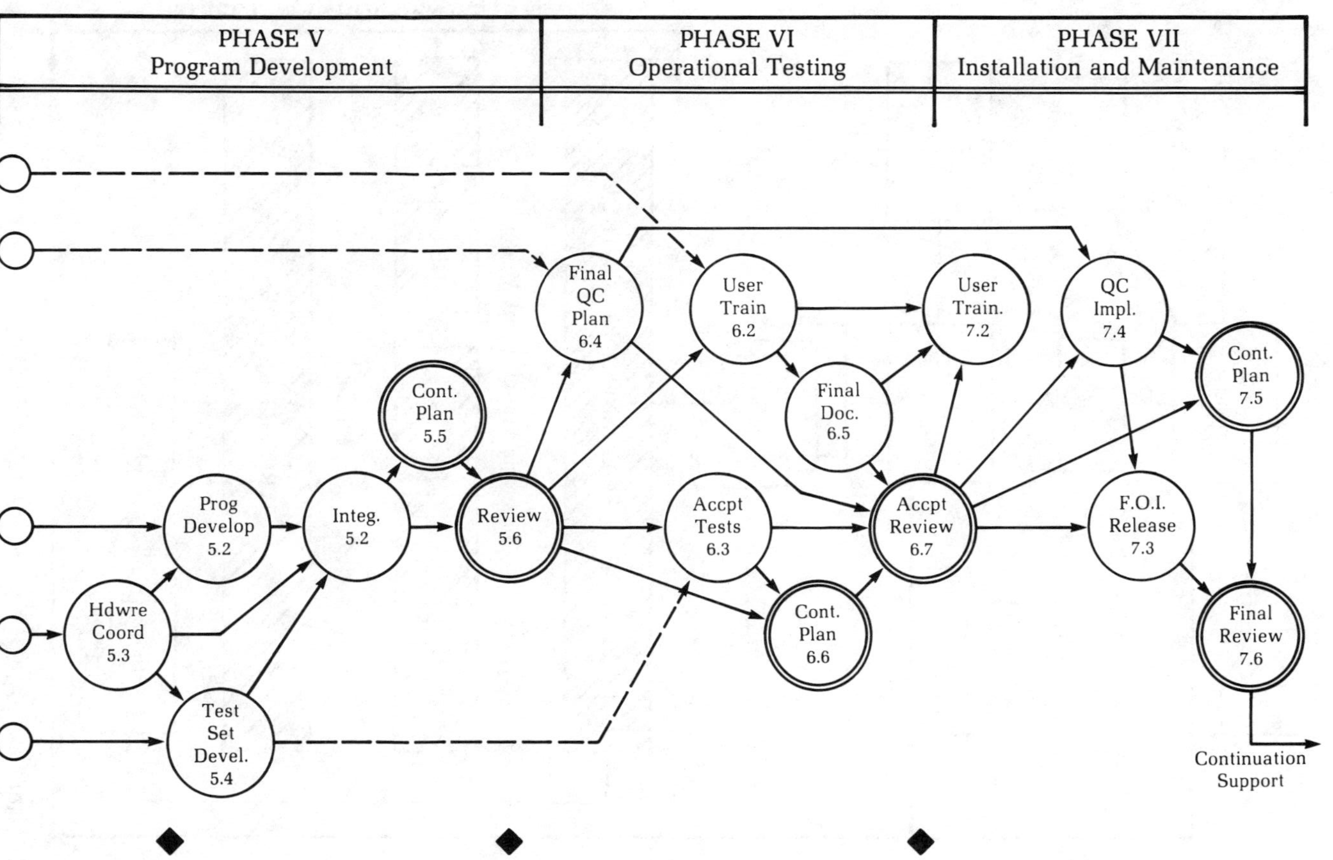
PHASE V
Program Development
PHASE VI
Operational Testing
PHASE VII
Installation and Maintenance
Prog
Develop
5.2
Hdwre
Coord
5.3
Test
Set
Devel.
5.4
Integ.
5.2
Cont.
Plan
5.5
Review
5.6
Final
QC
Plan
6.4
User
Train
6.2
Accpt
Tests
6.3
Final
Doc.
6.5
Cont.
Plan
6.6
Accpt
Review
6.7
User
Train.
7.2
QC
Impl.
7.4
F.O.I.
Release
7.3
Cont.
Plan
7.5
Final
Review
7.6
Continuation
Support

Information Requests
Long-Term Planning and Control
Constraints
Market
Technology
Economic
Development Plan
Resource Requirements
Maintenance/ Enhancement Requests
Mid-Term Planning and Control
Resources
Resource Acquisition
Resources
Priority List
Specific Project Proposals
PROJECT PLANNING AND CONTROL
Lifecycle Management Model
2
3
4
5
6
Phases
PROJECT REVIEW
Project Status Reports
Project Review Reports
PROJECT MANAGEMENT SYSTEM

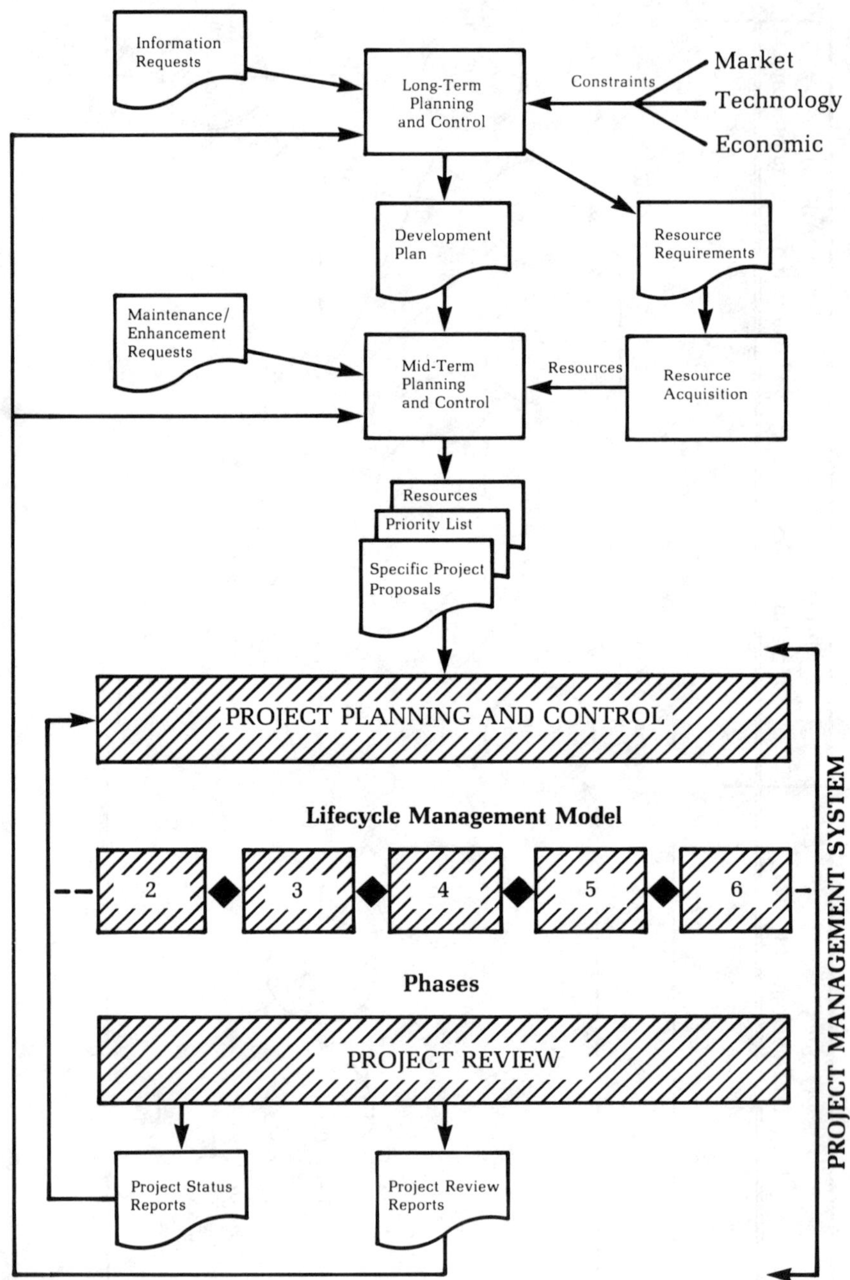

**Figure 3.2.**

Phase I, calling on technical expertise as needed. External assistant may be required.

I-2 *Problem Definition*

Entry into Phase I assumes that user requirements or a market study provide general project justification, or at lease Phase I justification. The first step in initiating any project must be describing the general problem to be solved. The result should be a brief but formal problem definition. Refer to Chapter 4 for details on developing this document.

I-3 *Initial Project Plan*

After the user (marketing management) agrees with the written problem definition, the next step is to develop an overall project plan showing critical path developments and a brief description of each research and development (R and D) problem that must be solved. Reasonably detailed cost estimates on Phase II must be prepared, possibly with minimum and maximum limits. Refer to Chapter 4 for details on developing this plan.

I-4 *Review*

It is necessary to conduct a formal review of the general project definition and plan as well as required changes by developer and user. Copies for reading and time for commenting should be provided before scheduled meetings. If the effort is justified, changes should be incorporated and the project should proceed to Phase II. Review should not terminate without countersignatures representing user and developer management agreement.

*Functional Analysis and Specification (Phase II)*

II-1 *Staffing*

Phase II requires the experience of people knowledgeable with the problem of user/costomer interface. User personnel must be dealt with carefully at all levels, and the analysis team must be groomed for marketing purposes. This is not the time to show off individual technical expertise or cleverness. The user must believe that his or her problems are in the hands of people who sincerely want to help. The use of outside expertise knowledgeable in the particular application area can be vital.

II-2 *Analysis of Overall System Functional Requirements*

Unless the user constrains particular hardware specifications (for example, a particular printer, modem, and so forth), hardware should remain unspecified. At this time the user should be encouraged to be completely open as to what is desired ideally as well as realistically. Obviously, the final system must lie between the present system and the ideal system. Refer to Chapter 5 for details on performing this step and the next. Everyone on the team should review this standard before performing any task.

II-3 *Development of Overall System Functional Specification*
This specification, in conjunction with the initial documentation set, should completely define the user functional requirements. No reference should be made to specific hardware types unless constrained. This must be a joint development effort with user personnel who will be involved in operating and using the existing system.

II-4 *Continuation Plan*
With the functional specifications completed, the overall project plan should be revised or refined, along with cost estimates and a detailed plan for Phase III.

II-5 *Review*
The last step of Phase II is to review specifications, plans, changes, and cost estimates with user/management, ensuring that total functional requirements are well defined and explained and that the plan is acceptable. If the effort is justified, changes should be incorporated, and the project should proceed to Phase III. Figure 3.3 illustrates schematically the project "tuning" that may result from a phase review. Incremental movements from each phase to another through a formal review "gate," enable potential project problems to be adjusted.

*Environment Analysis/Specification (Phase III)*

III-1 *Staffing*
Emphasis during this phase must be on the enlistment of highly qualified technical personnel, particularly in the advanced systems area. At least one person should be aware of the latest technology available. Real-world experience in a similar application area is also vital.

III-2 *Technology Analysis*
Existing hardware/software technology, applicability, and trade-offs should be analyzed to meet overall system functional specifications.

III-3 *Hardware Environment Synthesis*
The system hardware environment should be synthesized, on a building-block basis. For example, computer processors and peripherals for both the development and field environments should be selected.

III-4 *Software Environment Synthesis*
The system software environment should be synthesized, on a building-block basis. For example, operating system, language, and support software should be selected for both the development and field environments.

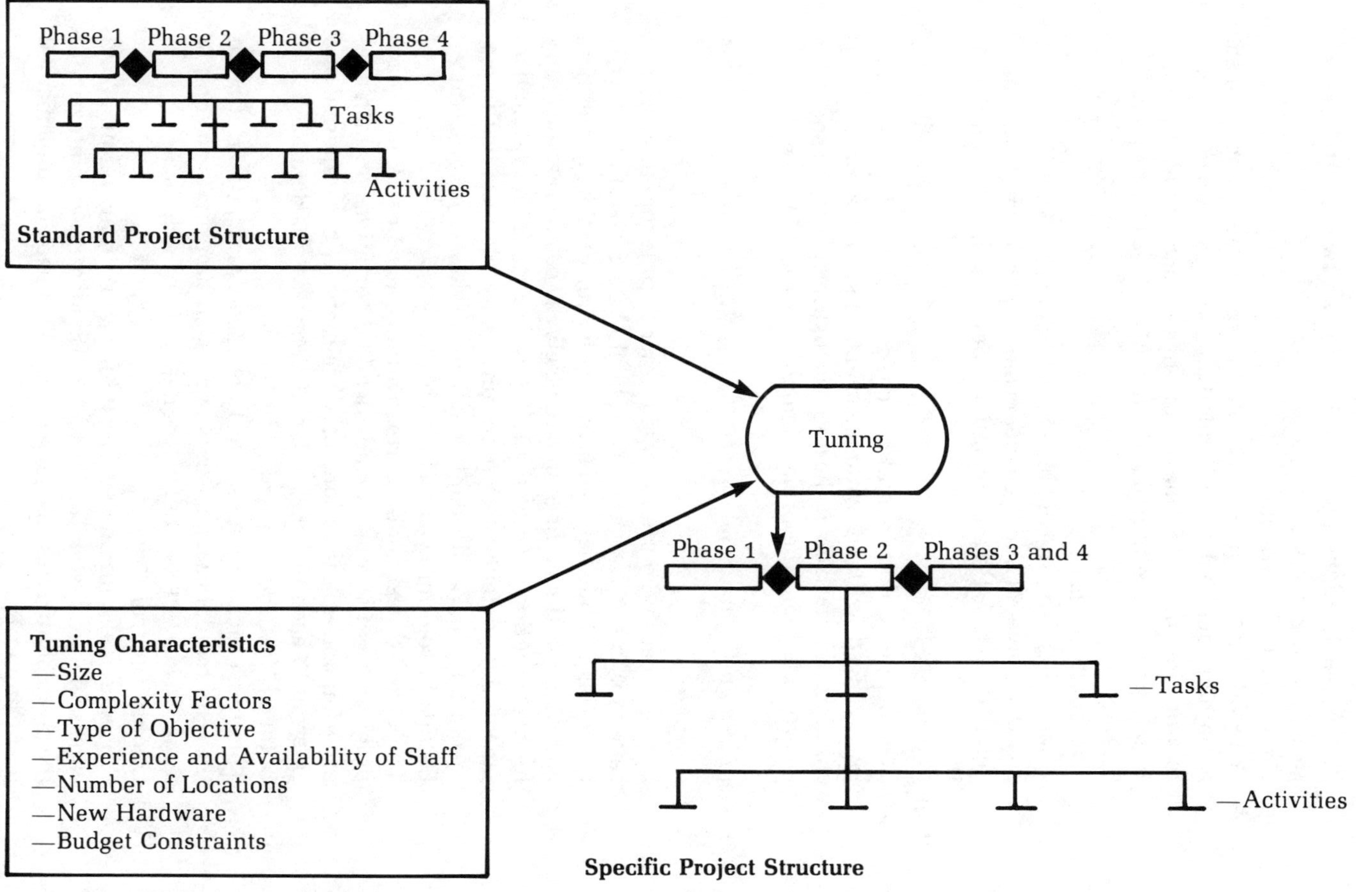


**Figure 3.3.** Phase Review "Tuning."

III-5 *Hardware/Software System Specifications*
These specifications should reflect the hardware/software synthesis requirements as stated above.

III-6 *Preliminary Documentation Set*
A detailed user's manual should be completed, along with the remaining detailed functional documentation, including system outline, output formats, data-base descriptions, and input formats. This preliminary documentation set is described in Chapter 5.

III-7 *Continuation Plan*
A more detailed project plan should be developed, nailing down any unresolved R and D elements along the critical path. A more detailed cost estimate should be developed, particularly for Phase IV.

III-8 *Review*
Specifications, documentation, changes, and estimates should be reviewed with user/management, ensuring a clear understanding of approach. If the effort is justified, changes should be incorporated and the project should proceed to Phase IV.

*System Design (Phase IV)*

IV-1 *Staffing*
Programmers who are expected to write code for subprograms called for in the system outline should be selected to help write the corresponding detailed program documentation. In addition, particular staff members should be given specific responsibility for coordinating each of the following areas: total system documentation, detailed test procedures and full cycle test implementation plan, and quality control standards and procedures.

IV-2 *Detailed Program Documentation*
The detailed design and corresponding documentation of each program module must include detailed narratives on each subprogram and specifications of all references, both internal and external to each module. Refer to Chapter 6 for details.

IV-3 *Detailed Test Plan*
This must include detailed test schedules and a description of the required data sets needed to test each subprogram as part of a regression test set. Refer to Chapter 8 for details.

IV-4 *Quality Control Plan*
Procedures should be developed for maintaining, refining, and enhancing the system, ensuring system identity and integrity of the product libraries as changes are developed and implemented (see Chapter 8).

IV-5 *Continuation Plan*
The final detailed continuation plan should include formal specifications, documentation, and cost estimates for the critical design review. Refer to Chapter 9 for details.

IV-6 *Critical Design Review*
The critical design review evaluates the continuation plan and required changes. At this point the user must be made to understand the potential level of difficulty of incorporating changes once program development (Phase V) is under way. A reasonable amount of time should be allowed for this review/revision period because of (1) level of complexity of the decisions at this time, (2) volume of documentation and corresponding effort for changes, and (3) fermentation period to allow review of how changes propagate through the system.

*Program Development (Phase V)*

V-1 *Staffing*
After the written, detailed system software documentation is reviewed, it may be desirable to shift personnel assignments. This is a critical decision step. It is most desirable that those designers who have written satisfactory documentation remain to supervise writing of the corresponding code. Poor documentation will generally indicate lack of understanding or the inability to supervise or write good code. Also, the personnel resources required to produce an adequate test set should not be underestimated.

V-2 *Program Development/Integration*
It will be necessary to coordinate emphasis on the development of critical path programs to facilitate proper test plan implementation. For example, it is necessary, to ensure construction of input edit and database update programs before accessing the database for processing and output.

V-3 *Hardware Facility Coordination*
Scheduling of required hardware facilities for compilation and testing may be crucial, depending on the environment for this phase. It is easy to accumulate day-by-day slippage owing to improper coordination of hardware test facilities, conversions, and so forth.

V-4 *Test Set Development*
As compilation gets underway, programming personnel should have gained sufficient knowledge and should have been provided sufficient time to develop detailed test procedures. In any event this time period must be planned in advance, with emphasis on

input interface and database maintenance programs to ensure database integrity. It is imperative at this time to isolate personnel responsibility for the coordination of detailed test procedures and materials for a regression test set to be used in whole or part each time the system is modified.

V-5 *Continuation Plan*

A detailed plan should be developed for operational testing (Phase VI), and plans for future phases should be refined. A detailed cost estimate should be developed for operational testing and for future phases. Sufficient resources should be included to ensure integrity of specifications and documentation for project intracommunications as well as user review. Plans for long-term system/product support and distribution should be developed at this time.

V-6 *Review*

Specifications, documentation, changes, plan, and estimates should be reviewed with user/management, ensuring clear understanding of system operation and the approach to projected effectiveness of the operational testing plan.

*Operational Testing (Phase VI)*

VI-1 *Staffing*

Direct management responsibility for coordination of operational testing should be assigned to a specific individual. The objective is the development of a set of full system tests with effectiveness that is satisfactory to both user and developer management. The responsibility for operational testing must be kept separate from completion of final documentation and coordination of user requests for review and modification.

VI-2 *User Personnel Training*

The user personnel training period provides the opportunity to "shake down" the documentation—for example, the user's manual and the operations manual—as well as the system itself. This period usually generates requests for modifications that should not be introduced without following formal procedures. Refer to Chapter 6 for performance of this and the next two steps.

VI-3 *Full-Cycle Acceptance Testing*

Final full-cycle acceptance testing must be performed with user personnel (or the equivalent) under simulated real-world conditions in order to be effective. For software products, initial versions usually can be given out at no cost to friendly users to accomplish real-life operational testing. Such user installations generally are known as alpha and beta test sites.

VI-4 *Quality Control Procedures*
Formal distribution and support procedures should be implemented. Finalized procedures for processing requests for corrections, refinements, and enhancements, must ensure a thorough understanding of both user and developer management regarding the generation of new versions and releases.

VI-5 *Final Documentation*
Additions to the documentation set that depend on final program construction must be incorporated at this time. Assignment of this function to someone other than the originating programmer can be an effective method for review of internal documentation, programming practices, and skill, as well as the detailed external documentation.

VI-6 *Continuation Plan*
A detailed plan should be developed for cutover to installation and support (Phase VII), and any future plans should be outlined. Cost estimates should be included for steady-state operation as well as for the initial period. Allowances for formal modification procedures should be included as should recovery procedures to cover (1) on-site restart and (2) abort and return to operational testing phase.

VI-7 *Review and Acceptance*
This is the final review and acceptance of documentation, changes, plan, and estimates for installation and support with user and developer management. Emphasis is on recovery, maintenance, and modification procedures. Written approval and schedule to proceed should be obtained.

*Installation and Support (Phase VII)*

VII-1 *Staffing*
Staff considerations during Phase VII include users in selecting any additional personnel required beyond those participating in operational testing, shifting present personnel where desirable, and selecting personnel for user training. The developer should assist the user in selecting user interface as well as on-site or on-call personnel for system support and in evaluating requirements for implementing and controlling product library changes. Ample time should be allowed for this step and the next before system production begins.

VII-2 *User Personnel Training/Guidance*
Off-site as well as on-site classroom sessions should be provided for all personnel, both user and support. Ongoing training for new and backup personnel should be considered.

VII-3 *Full Operation Implementation/Product Release*

Timing and coordination usually are critical. Plans must include abort timing and corresponding personnel activity or nonactivity. Revovery procedures should be well documented and understood.

VII-4 *Quality Control Implementation*

Formal support procedures are required to determine responsibility for system errors and the corresponding correction process. Notification for correction requests can be initiated by the system support agent as well as the user. The divergence of identity of multiple fielded systems can prove catastrophic in most applications; its avoidance depends on well-disciplined support procedures to ensure congruence. Formal procedures for processing requests for system refinements and enhancements are necessary to ensure that required resources are scoped properly and that allowance is included for preserving system identity and integrity of the product libraries. A detailed set of procedures is described in Chapter 9. Accumulating modification requests is desirable as long as the system remains operable so that total documentation and program modification efforts can be grouped into new releases. Quality control procedures should be strictly followed for all modifications that are under direct management responsibility for process and approval. The objective is to ensure reliable operation within an effective test bed, simulating real-world conditions before each new release. Continual refinement of the regression test set and corresponding documentation will afford procedures that are easily implemented and controlled.

VII-5 *Continuation Plan*

The level of continuation planning required depends on the level of activity and scope of modification requests. Plans will fall into three basic categories: hold, implement, and major system rewrite. Major modifications should be initiated at an effective phase and developed in accordance with successive phases as applicable. Major system rewrites should start back at Phase I.

VII-6 *Review*

The level and formality of reviews depends on continuation plan activity. In any event, formal user/management reviews should be undertaken at least once annually.

# CHAPTER 4

# Project Definition

## 4.1 OVERVIEW

The decision to develop a new software system should be supported by three major activities: (1) a product request, (2) definition of the development problem, and (3) a project development plan. The prime mover for most development projects is a formal request for a product to meet a particular need. The request may come from an organization within the developer's company (for example, marketing or product planning). It may also be a request for proposal (RFP) received from an outside organization (for example, a customer). These two types of systems are described in Chapter 1. The request typically specifies the various requirements and characteristics of the desired product and thereby presents the developer with a problem to be solved. Before it can be solved, however, the problem must be analyzed and systematically defined in simple but formal terms. The problem definition documentation describes in essence *what* is to be produced. Once the problem is formally identified and defined, a project plan is developed that defines *how* the product is to be produced. This chapter addresses these two major steps that lead to the establishment of a development project. In particular, the chapter presents guidelines for defining a system development project from a set of given requirements.

## 4.2 PROBLEM DEFINITION

The problem definition procedure should produce a three-to-five page document that clearly defines the overall problem and the ground rules for its solution. It is management's responsibility to ensure that this formal written problem definition is properly maintained during the entire project lifetime; any ground rule changes must be incorporated immediately. This process will tend to emphasize the effect of changing ground rules and the importance of a solid problem definition foundation at the beginning.

### Format

The format elements to be followed for a formal problem definition are: (1) objective, (2) constraints, (3) external parameters, (4) internal parameters, and (5) strategy. An explanation of each is given.

1. *Objective:* The overall problem objective should be stated simply and clearly in one or two sentences. An objective may be a fixed goal or set of goals. More often, it entails the optimization of some performance characteristic. If optimization is involved, only one function can be maximized (minimized). This function may be a weighted combination of subfunctions, but the weighting must be defined. Constraints, parameters, or strategy as defined below should not be included in the statement of objective.

2. *Constraints:* List all constraints that must be adhered to during the project lifetime. If constraints vary with time, state how they vary and their applicable time periods.

3. *External parameters:* List all parameters that can affect problem solutions but for which little control exists. These parameters must be monitored as the project proceeds because they can affect strategy.

4. *Internal parameters:* List all parameters that can affect problem solution and on which reasonable control can be exercised. These are the parameters that management controls to effect the strategy.

5. *Strategy:* Set down the overall strategy to be used to solve the problem as defined. This should be a brief step-by-step narrative in general terms. It should not be a detailed plan.

The resultant problem definition document should serve to "clear the air" with higher management in a gross sense. Therefore there should be no "unmentioned" objectives, constraints, or parameters. In fact, this is the place to document controversial influences on strategy.

### Project Development Categories

The problem definition process will identify the project to be in either of two categories:

1. *Software only development:* Many system requirements can be met totally by development of software to be operated either on the requester's existing computing equipment or on mature computing equipment to be obtained from a vendor other than the developer.

2. *Hardware/software development:* In some situations the development problem solution can only be realized by functional trade-offs between hardware and software system components. These cases often imply concurrent development of the hardware and the software. Such projects require that careful consideration be given to coordination of the dependent milestones of the two development efforts and to intercommunication between two often disparate technical disciplines.

## 4.3 SAMPLE PROBLEM DEFINITION

### Objective

Develop the software for an interactive data entry system that can be used to compose complex transactions on keyboard/display terminals for all major data entry applications within the company. Include the development of software to automate conversion of new applications.

### Constraints

1. Develop the required software using the incremental method, from problem definition through the installation and support phase.
2. The customer sales system will be the starting application; the warehouse system will be the second application.
3. Both applications will be made fully operational under this project. Other applications will be accounted for in the design.
4. The system must be interface compatible with present file-management and retrieval subsystems.
5. A major design consideration is the use of local minicomputers to house the interactive data entry system and drive keyboard/display terminals.
6. The software for each application should be considered as separate systems running independently, possibly on separate minicomputers.

7. The system will be developed and maintained under the main computer time-sharing system using all development and maintenance tools available.
8. The system will be written entirely in COBOL under a standard that ensures operation on at least two competitively available minicomputers, with language support for up to five terminals operating simultaneously.
9. The operational cost (including maintenance) of the system on a minicomputer configuration should not exceed the cost of operation for the two initial applications, including write-off of the development over an eight-year period.
10. The software development and start-up costs should not exceed $600,000. This includes all costs and overhead associated with personnel, computer time, external purchases, and so forth. Cost of minicomputers, terminals, and the like will be considered elsewhere.
11. The length of the project, from start of functional specification to end of operational testing should not exceed 18 months.

## External Parameters

1. Available work done elsewhere on similar systems.
2. Availability of minicomputers having the required application environment support software, particularly the interactive, reentrant COBOL.
3. Compatability of the time-sharing development environment with the minicomputer operational environment.
4. User limitations on personnel to assist in the various phases of this project.
5. Availability of outside expertise, particularly in the minicomputer area.

## Internal Parameters

1. Availability of experienced personnel knowledgeable in the various development areas required, particularly in user application areas.
2. Ability to hire new personnel with required special expertise.
3. Ability to train existing personnel in new areas; availability of funds for training.
4. Availability of funds for contractual and/or consulting assistance.
5. Availability of funds for hardware/software purchases.

**Strategy**

1. Finalize problem definition and develop overall project plan.
2. Analyze and specify in detail the functional requirements of the two applications to be accommodated. Also consider the special requirements of other potential applications for implementation and conversion.
3. Analyze and specify the hardware/software requirements of the two applications to be accommodated for both the application and development environments. Consider the other potential applications.
4. Design the system and produce the external documentation set, a plan for testing, and a plan for quality control.
5. Construct the system and test bed environment.
6. Implement the system under a parallel test environment.
7. Cut over to live operation when reliability confidence levels are acceptable.

## 4.4 PROJECT PLANNING

### General Considerations

Software project planning is fraught with a multitude of hazards that can ensure disaster at the outset of the project. Typically, the uninitiated user places the same confidence in the software developer that he would in the architect who designs his building. Just as typical is the rude awakening that has resulted as many projects have progressed toward completion. Time schedules have been pushed back, costs increased, and functional capability cut.

Almost all software project failures result from poor project planning. Poor planning is, of course, due to bad judgment and inexperienced management. Why do these problems seem to prevail in the software field? Alternatively, what constituents of accurate project plans have produced successful software products.

To answer these two questions, we must start with the realization that a plan is simply a set of milestones leading to project completion, along with estimates of the time and resources required to achieve the milestones. It does not take a good manager to list a set of sensible milestones or a logical path to project completion. Therefore the problem lies in estimating and controlling the time and resources required to achieve the milestones successfully. To understand why the software estimation problem is so difficult, let us look at what is required to produce estimates (forecasts) in general.

Estimation and forecasting depend on a knowledge of the past. If a software developer does not have a good "corporate memory" covering many case histories, then the data on which to base a future estimate does not exist. In addition, estimation and forecasting require skillful interpretation of past histories in terms of present problem definitions. Without this experience past history cannot be properly used.

Lack of a good corporate memory within the software industry has at least three causes. First, the field of major software product development is quite young, about 20 years old. Second, software generally has been purchased with "soft" dollars as opposed to "hard" dollars. Most software either has been delivered with the hardware or developed "inhouse." Inhouse personnel and machine time are wasted with low visibility, as opposed to hard dollars. Third, when a hardware product is killed, the "remains" usually stand around for years so that people may observe the hard lessons learned. The pieces of hardware that were purchased are now visible as a wasted ensemble that renders all the expensive components worthless. Software, on the other hand, may simply sit in the corner as a pile of so much paper, whose value is intrinsically negligible. In this state a line of code has no recognizable value to most people.

Successfully managed software products usually occur in those environments wherein a developer is paid hard dollars by the customer who is purchasing a software product as a stand-alone item. The cost as well as the shortcomings of such a product are highly visible. The incremental method presented here has been developed in such an environment.

## Cost Estimation Techniques

The accurate prediction of costs and development time for software projects has been a longstanding problem. Volumes of horror stories can be cited, telling of massive cost overruns and of projects delayed by years, or never completed at all. Many of these fiascos derived from "hip-shooting" estimates that invariably were grossly optimistic. The basic problem was a general lack of understanding of the nature and mechanisms of software management and an exploding new industry growing faster than its disciplines.

Since the early 1970s several schemes and methodologies have been developed by various persons who recognized the problem. Today, the software development cycle is well defined and is steadily becoming understood and accepted, with standard practices by the industry. These standards, in turn, are serving as the foundation for systematic approaches to the problem of accurately and dependably estimating software development projects.

Table 4.1 summarizes several current cost-estimating methods, showing the inherent advantages and disadvantages of each. Most of today's

**TABLE 4.1** Comparative Micro Estimation Methods

| *Item* | *Method Name* | *Estimating Technique* | *Advantages* | *Disadvantages* |
|---|---|---|---|---|
| 1 | Top down | Based on total cost of large portions of previous projects | Simple, fast, convenient | Risk of overlooking embedded special or difficult technical problems; lack of details for cost justifications |
| 2 | Ratio Estimating | Break down to smallest possible modules, estimate lines of code and relative complexity per module, apply empirical programmer productivity rate | Simple, fast, convenient | Suffers from the need for a valid cost data base for many diverse estimating situations |
| 3 | Standards estimating | Based on performance standards that have been systematically developed, Standards used as stable reference points | Convenient, consistent, accurate for repeating operations | Not accurate unless the same operations are performed repeatedly |
| 4 | Bottom up | Total job broken down into small work packages and work units and assigned to appropriate technical talents for bidding; incremental estimates then combined into a total package cost | Can be distributed to the people who will do the work | Total cost of the project not immediately in perspective; estimator not sensitive to the reasonableness of the total software package cost |

*Source:* Ware Myers, "A Statistical Approach to Scheduling Software Development," *Computer*, December 1978.

conventional methods can be considered *micro estimating* techniques in which the estimations are derived from a detailed internal analysis of the proposed project. These techniques typically decompose the project into the smallest definable set of modules (or tasks), estimate the number of source statements (or lines of code) for each module, and apply an empirically based programmer productivity rate to obtain an incremental estimate of the project effort (man months or man years). The estimate is then converted to dollars by the application of prevailing labor rates. These methods are generally effective for small projects involving a total of 10,000 or fewer lines of code and requiring a small cadre of programmers to implement. For larger projects involving several years of development and a large programming staff, the estimation errors inherent in the micro estimating methods often become prohibitive.

For large projects a *macro estimating* technique has evolved that attempts to forecast manpower and schedule directly from estimators available at the start of design. Certain macro methods are based on empirical evidence that the software lifecycle pattern can be effectively fitted by the Rayleigh equation as a model (Putnam, 1976). A further realization has been made that the area under the Rayleigh curve represents the total manpower expenditure for the lifecycle. Applying the incremental method to the Rayleigh model consists of segmenting the model by the incremental phases and successively predicting the manpower requirements from the overall lifecycle model. Once the area under the curve is determined by, say, the experience of completing Phase II, successive phase manpower estimates can become almost mechanical, using the equation of the model and standards to measure milestone completion. An advantage of the macro estimating technique is that managers are estimating with parameters they are comfortable with—manpower and time. No unfamiliar data processing jargon is involved. A disadvantage is to rely too mechanically on the accuracy of the Rayleigh model and the standards. An example is given at the end of Section 4.6.

## 4.5 THE INCREMENTAL PLAN

For any sizable software development, it is impossible to produce an accurate, detailed estimate for the entire project during the project definition phase. The exception is the case when the same team is developing a similar software product for a similar customer environment under similar circumstances. Even the conversion of an identical software product to a different machine has, in many cases, been an unpredictable nightmare.

Because new software developments can have estimation errors of the order of hundreds of percents, a satisfactory method for project evolution is the incremental plan, in which resources and funds are committed in small pieces. This approach appears to satisfy estimation shortcomings, benefiting both user and developer. First, it is not difficult to convince a customer that costs for the individual pieces are no more expensive when purchased separately. The only additional expenses are the cost of documenting the work done to date, and the time needed to review it. This is essentially the cost of an insurance policy. If the customer does not like the initial pieces that are produced, he can stop before becoming too committed. The developer, on the other hand, can be more realistic, showing what the customer needs as opposed to restating what the customer thinks he will get.

In any case, the incremental approach forces a detailed, accurate forecast and estimate of the overall project by splitting it into finer pieces. The following points are offered to aid in developing the project plan.

1. *Time phase milestones.* Using the time phase milestones set down in the management plan as a guide, list those that are pertinent to the particular project at hand. Include additional milestones that are a result of the special properties of the project. Such milestones may include special hardware or support software developments, procurements, or special conversions to be performed.

2. *Critical path unknowns.* Critical path unknowns are those items on the critical path of development that require research and development or are ill defined. If in doubt, leave it in! Now is the time to air any dirty laundry.

3. *Critical path lead time requirements.* List those items along the critical path that require lead time because of external requirements. For example, hardware procurements may require initiation many months before delivery. Conversions may have to be initiated months before the requirement for a good data base. Allow time for special training of personnel where required.

4. *Time and cost estimates.* Preliminary time schedules for the development of any major software product should be estimated with minimum and maximum time projections to account for unknowns. It is not unusual for "worst-case" estimates to be well exceeded.

Preliminary resource projections should be estimated separately for each elementary item on the time schedule. Refer to the sample initial project plan contained in the next section.

## 4.6 SAMPLE INITIAL PROJECT PLAN

This initial project plan describes the rough overall plan, time phase milestone (TPM) cost estimates, and critical path unknowns for solving the problem specified in the problem definition for this system. The incremental method will be applied for managing and controlling the project.

This initial project plan was developed on the assumption that the applications systems would not be substantially changed beyond their present state. Review of similar system developments indicates that if additional complexities were added, the gross costs could be expanded by 100 to 200% of the projections in this plan. The Phase II projections should be accurate to within 10%.

With the incremental method, resources will be committed on a firm basis for only one phase at a time and only after each phase has been carefully planned and reviewed.

## Time Phase Milestones

The time phase milestones for this project are outlined as steps within phases. Steps may proceed concurrently or be interchanged in order. Phases will proceed sequentially, in strict order, with no overlap. Successive phases will not be initiated unless careful review clearly demonstrates sufficient justification and preparation. The phases and milestones are given below.

*Problem Definition/Planning (Phase I)*

I-1 *Problem Definition*
This document represents results of this step.

I-2 *Initial Project Plan*
This document represents results of this step.

I-3 *Review*
Review the problem definition and initial project plan with user representatives and development managers. Initiation of Phase II is contingent on an agreement by both parties accepting both the project definition and project plan.

*Functional Analysis/Specification (Phase II)*

II-1 *Analysis of System Functional Requirements*
Analyze the functional requirements of the two applications selected, using the system analysis standard as a guide. This will require a commitment of user personnel time for working with the system analysis team.

II-2 *Development of System Functional Specifications*
Develop jointly, with the user representatives, the software system functional specifications as defined in the functional specification standards described in Section 5.8.

a. Analyze and document outputs: Mock up, in example form, output messages, reports, and the input query that initiated the output. Then describe all the possible entries of all fields in the input and output messages. Make an ordered list of all fields used in the output messages. This list will also contain references to the output messages where these fields are utilized.

b. Analyze and document inputs/prompting: Mock up input messages, in example form. Describe all fields that comprise the input messages. Design and document all prompting for the data elements, including descriptions of the prompting as necessary. Establish audit trails from fields to messages as well as data elements to fields. Document an example of the complete prompting for at least one message.

c. Analyze and document performance requirements: Analyze and document the mapping of inputs to data base and data base to outputs. Provide a stationary as well as a time dependent audit trail of these. Document response time of outputs and inputs as well as frequency of use for both.

II-3 *Continuation Plan*

When the system functional specifications are complete, refine or revise the overall project plan along with TPM cost estimates and a detailed plan for Phase III.

II-4 *Review*

Review specifications, plans, changes, and TPM cost estimates with user representatives and management. Ensure that the total functional requirements are well defined and fully understood. If the effort is justified and plans are accepted, proceed to Phase III.

*Environment Analysis/Specification (Phase III)*

III-1 *Technology Analysis*

Analyze the availability of existing minicomputer technology (that is, hardware, operating systems, COBOL compilers, support software) and its applicability to meet requirements. Evaluate trade-offs to meet overall system functional specifications.

hardware, operating systems, COBOL compilers, support software) and its applicability to meet requirements. Evaluate trade-offs to meet overall system functional specifications.

III-2 *Hardware Environment Synthesis*

Synthesize, on a building-block basis, system hardware (that is, selection of minicomputer, memory requirements, and peripherals) for both the development and application environments.

III-3 *Software Environment Synthesis*
Synthesize, on a building-block basis, system software (that is, compiler, operating system components and support software components) for both the development and application environments.

III-4 *Initial Documentation Set*
Develop the documentation required to complete the functional and environment specifications, using the documentation standard. The initial documentation set will include a detailed users manual, system overview, human interface specifications, database specifications, and communication specifications.

III-5 *Continuation Plan*
Develop a more detailed project plan, firming up any unresolved elements along the critical path. Develop a more detailed TPM cost estimate. Develop a detailed plan for Phase IV.

III-6 *Review*
Review specifications, documentation, changes, and estimates with user representatives and management, ensuring a clear understanding of approach. If effort is justified and plans are accepted, proceed to Phase IV.

*System Design (Phase IV)*

IV-1 *Detailed Program Documentation*
Design and document in complete detail each program module, using the documentation standard as a guide.

IV-2 *Detailed Test Plan*
Develop detailed test procedures and descriptions of the data sets needed to test each subprogram. Develop a plan for priority testing of all subprograms based on data-set dependency.

IV-3 *Quality Control Plan*
Develop procedures for maintaining, refining, and enhancing the system that will ensure system and documentation integrity as modifications are developed and implemented. Use the quality control standard as a guide.

IV-4 *Continuation Plan*
Develop a final detailed design plan including refinement of the formal specifications, documentation, and TPM cost estimates for critical design review.

IV-5 *Critical Design Review*
Review the continuation plan and make required changes. Because of the potential level of difficulty of incorporating changes once the development phase is initiated, allot a reasonable period to this review in consideration of the following factors:

a. Level of overall system complexity

b. Volume of documentation and corresponding effort for change
c. Fermentation of changes to allow review of their propagation through the system

*Program Development (Phase V)*

V-1 *Hardware Facility Preparation*
Procure and prepare hardware facilities needed to complete the development and test the system.

V-2 *Program Development*
Develop programs based on the detailed program documentation and the programming standard.

V-3 *Module Testing*
Construct test data in parallel with program development in accordance with the testing/quality control standard.

V-4 *System Integration*
Implement detailed test procedures as critical path subprograms clear compilation. Develop and document the regression test set. Implement corresponding test procedures as system integration proceeds.

V-5 *Integration Testing*
Implement integration test plans and procedures. Develop a detailed plan for operational test implementation, along with detailed cost estimates for future phases.

V-6 *Review*
Review the specifications, documentation, changes, and estimates with user representatives and management. If integration testing has been completed satisfactorily, proceed with Phase VI.

*Operational Test (Phase VI)*

VI-1 *User Personnel Training*
Train user personnel to use the interactive display terminals. Use this training period to shake down the documentation set, as well as the system in general.

VI-2 *Quality Control Procedures*
Document formal quality control procedures in accordance with system maintenance requirements and the quality control standard.

VI-3 *Full-Cycle Acceptance Testing*
Perform the final full-cycle acceptance test with user personnel or the equivalent under real conditions.

VI-4 *Documentation and Test Sets*
Finalize the system documentation and regression test sets in accordance with their respective standards.

VI-5 *Continuation Plan*
Prepare a detailed plan for cutover to live operation. Prepare cost estimates for steady state operation as well as the initial cutover period. Develop recovery procedures for (1) restart, and (2) abort and return to operational test phase.

VI-6 *Review*
Perform a final review with all user personnel and development management before going live.

*Installation and Support (Phase VII)*

VII-1 *User Personnel Training*
Provide on-site training sessions for all personnel, including user management and maintenance personnel.

VII-2 *Full Operation Implementation*
Bring full system into live operation under close developer surveillance for at least one month.

VII-3 *Full Quality Control Implementation*
Invoke final maintenance procedures under the close surveillance of developer personnel for a period of at least one month.

VII-4 *Continuation Plan*
Write this document during the first month of live operation.

VII-5 *Final Review*
Carry out a final review with both user and developer management to cover the entire system development cycle and discuss what can be done to improve new or similar software system implementations. Cover further planning for this system, and set dates for additional formal reviews.

## Time and Cost Estimates

Preliminary time schedules for the development of the interactive data entry/retrieval system are shown in Figure 4.1. It must be emphasized, except for Phase II, that these projections may be highly inaccurate because of lack of detailed knowledge of the system requirements, as well as the critical path unknowns at this point. Nonetheless, these projections are considered to be the best estimates at this time.

Preliminary manpower resource projections are tabulated below by project phase. These resource projections are given in more detail (in terms of number of technical persons required) on the individual time projection sheets in figures 4.1 through 4.8 (the numbers above the time-span lines correspond to the number of persons required).

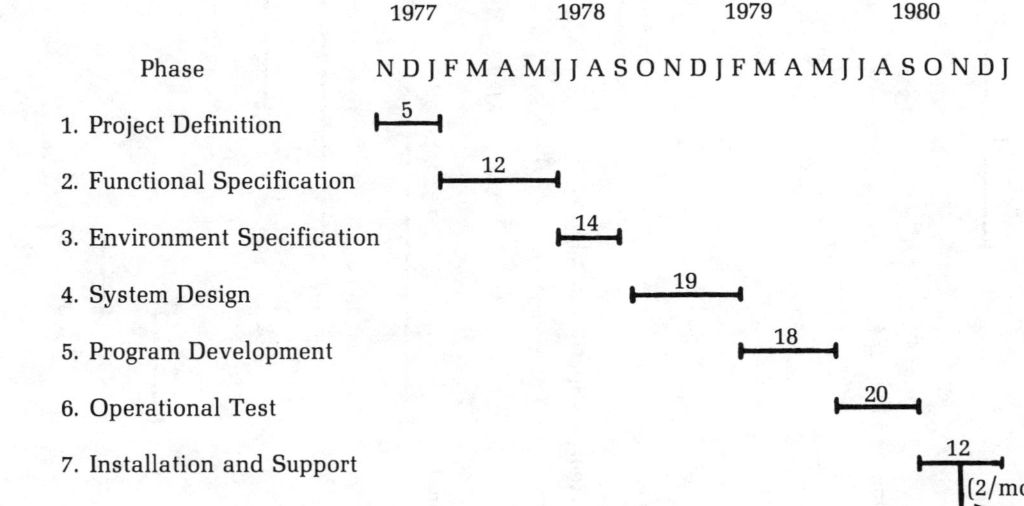


*These numbers represent total project man-months to be expended during each phase.

**Figure 4.1.** Overall Resource Schedule.

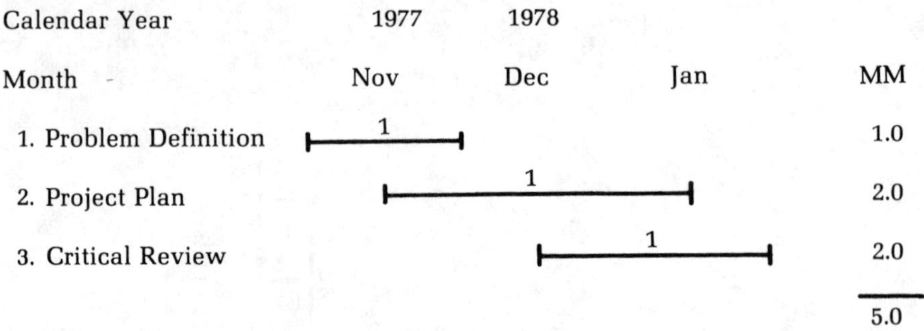


**Figure 4.2.** Project Definition Phase.

**Figure 4.3.** Functional Analysis/Specification Phase.

| Calendar Year | 1978 | |
|---|---|---|
| Month | Feb Mar Apr May Jun | MM |
| 1. Analysis of Functional Requirements | Feb – Apr | |
| 2. Develop Functional Specifications | Mar – May | |
| 3. Continuation Plan | May – Jun | |
| 4. Review | May – Jun | |
| a. Initialization | 2 | 2.0 |
| b. First Pass | 2 | 2.0 |
| c. Second Pass | 3 | 3.0 |
| d. Documentation | 2 | 2.0 |
| e. Finalization | 1 | 2.0 |
| f. Review | 1 | 1.0 |
| | | 12.0 |

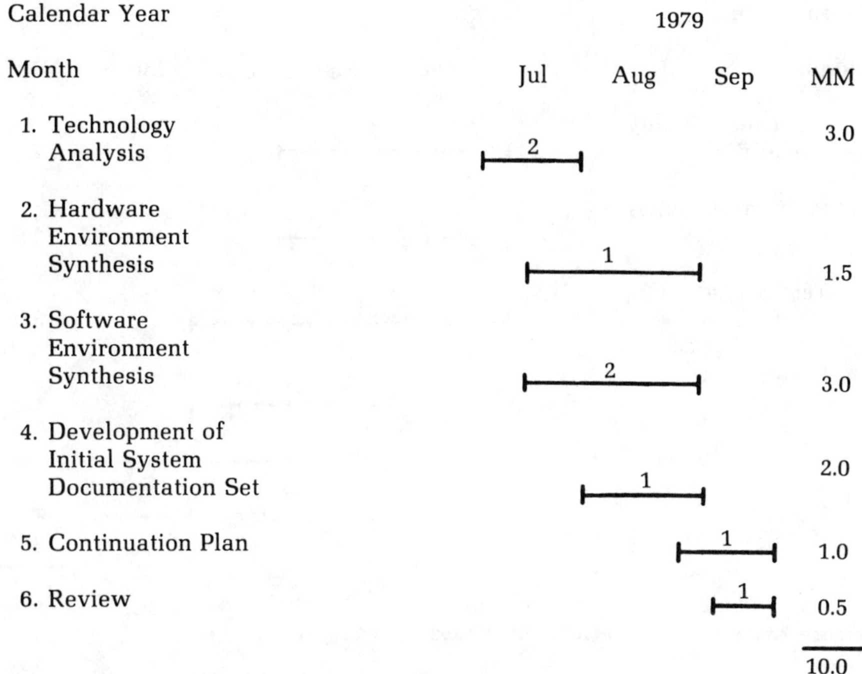


**Figure 4.4.** Environment Analysis/Specification.

**Figure 4.5.** System Design Phase.

| Calendar Year | 1978 | | 1979 | | |
|---|---|---|---|---|---|
| Month | Oct | Nov | Dec | Jan | MM |
| 1. Develop Detailed Program Documentation | | 3 | | | 12.0 |
| 2. Develop Detailed Test Plan | | | 1 | | 3.0 |
| 3. Develop Quality Control Plan | | | 1 | | 1.0 |
| 4. Continuation Plan | | | | 1 | 2.0 |
| 5. Critical Design Review | | | | 1 | 1.0 |
| | | | | | 19.0 |

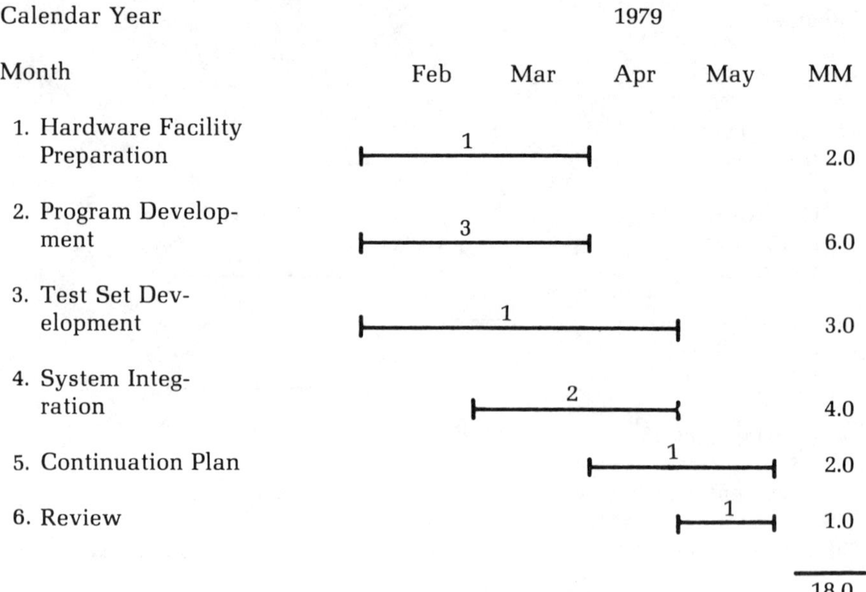


**Figure 4.6.** Program Development Phase.

**Figure 4.7.** Operational Test Phase.

Calendar Year 1979

| Month | Jun – Jul – Aug – Sep | MM |
|---|---|---|
| 1. User Personnel Training | 2 | 2.0 |
| 2. Implementation of Quality Control Procedure | 1 | 4.0 |
| 3. Full Cycle Acceptance Testing | 2 | 8.0 |
| 4. Finalize the Documentation and Test Sets | 2 | 4.0 |
| 5. Continuation Plan | 1 | 1.0 |
| 6. Review | 1 | 1.0 |
| | | 20.0 |

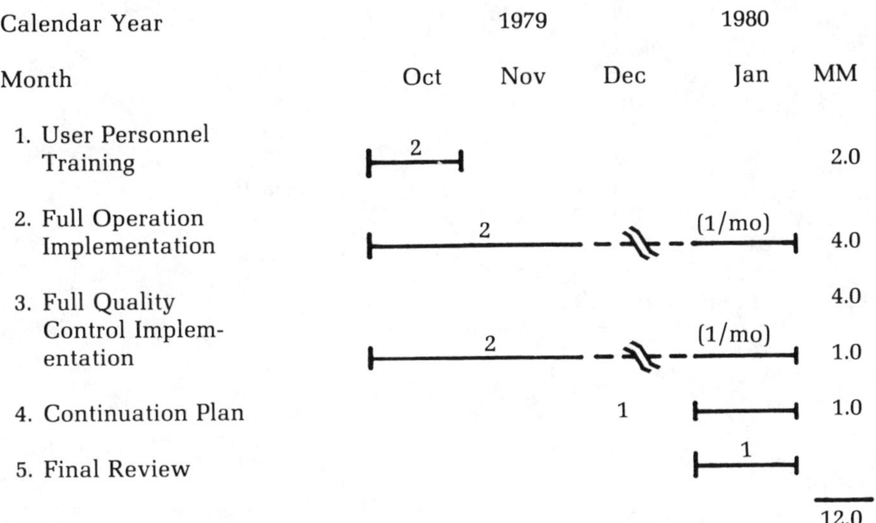


**Figure 4.8.** Installation and Support.

**Figure 4.9.** Incremental System Evolution.

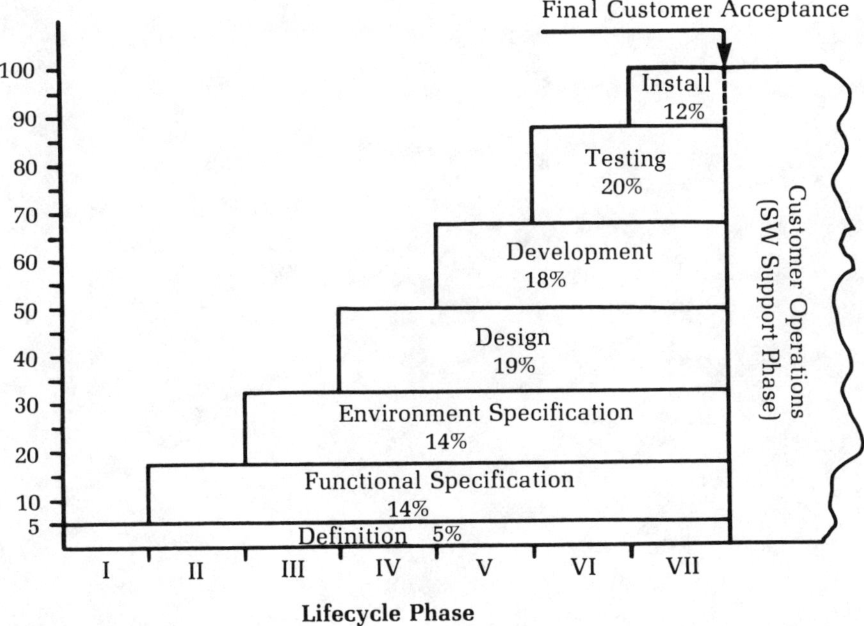

| *Phase* | *Man Months* | *% of total* |
|---|---|---|
| I | 5 | 5.0 |
| II | 12 | 12.0 |
| III | 14 | 14.0 |
| IV | 19 | 19.0 |
| V | 18 | 18.0 |
| VI | 20 | 20.0 |
| VII | 12 | 12.0 |
| | 100 | 100.0 |

Figure 4.9 shows graphically the incremental system evolution.

# CHAPTER 5

# System Functional Analysis and Specification

## 5.1 INTRODUCTION

This chapter provides procedures and standards for an organized approach to the functional analysis of a system to be automated. This analysis period is one in which persons experienced in systems automation must assimilate the knowledge of persons familiar with the functional requirements of an application system. The knowledge must then be organized in a manner that affords synthesis of an automated system. The total task is usually difficult, because the assimilation process meets with many natural resistances that stem from observation and interview of people who are responsible for performing daily tasks. If the level of automation experience is low, the process of organizing knowledge about the system can be tedious.

Nevertheless, the systems analysis process forms the foundation for development of any automated system. It must be performed thoroughly and correctly or the development process can go *out of control*. If not performed in an organized manner, within a reasonably short time period, the systems analysis process can stagnate with indecision. The purpose of the guidelines presented in this chapter is to assist in the production of a document that clearly specifies the system functional requirements in a manner amenable to automation, avoiding traditional pitfalls along the way.

## 5.2 BACKGROUND RATIONALE

Anyone engaged in systems analysis probably has encountered most of the following typical problems:

- Identifying proper user personnel or representatives to be interviewed
- Obtaining proper authority/approval to question them
- Getting full cooperation of user personnel on an individual basis during the interview period
- Getting full cooperation of user personnel on a group basis to gather statistics
- Getting user personnel to organize their thinking and provide constructive ideas that can be helpful to the automation process
- Getting user personnel to carefully review documents written by the analysis team to clarify functional requirements

In addition, someone from the analyzing organization must be concerned with the following problems:

- Controlling technical support personnel assigned to the analysis task, particularly the manner in which they interface with user personnel
- Ensuring that a well-planned, well-organized approach is taken throughout so that user personnel time is minimized, and certainly not wasted
- Resolving personality clashes that may occur between analysts and user personnel

All of these problems can be avoided, for the most part, by *establishing control at the outset* of the analysis phase and maintaining it throughout. The approach is a five-step process aimed at establishing and maintaining control and optimizing the effectiveness of personnel time:

1. *Initialization:* a period set aside at the outset to establish control and lay plans
2. *First Pass:* the initial round of scheduled interviews with user personnel
3. *Second pass:* the final round of scheduled interviews with user personnel
4. *Documentation:* a period for formal written description of the system functional requirements
5. *Finalization:* a period for formal agreement of user personnel on the written specifications

These steps are described in more detail in subsequent sections. Experience indicates that two distinct, well-planned passes with the user avoids divergence of requirements and diffusion into stagnant indecision, the two major pitfalls during the functional analysis and specification phase.

In addition to organizing and scheduling the system analysis specification, one must face the task of documentation. It is extremely important at the outset that everyone knows precisely what documents are to evolve during this phase. The workbook approach is not recommended, for it tends to cloud the top-level organization of the documentation. To emphasize the relationship between documents to be developed during this phase, as well as to provide insight into their evolution, we have described them separately (see Section 5.8).

## 5.3 INITIALIZATION

The initialization period is a time to establish control, lay plans, select personnel, and read background material. On formal approval of the systems analysis and specification phase, the following functions should be performed.

1. *Establish internal control.* Establish control of the system analysis team via formal memorandum from internal management as to team leader and starting personnel.

2. *Establish external control.* Establish control of the system analysis plan via formal letter or memorandum from user top management acknowledging responsibility, providing authority guidelines and introductory statements, and asserting the import and usefulness intended. This memorandum should be jointly prepared. It should be drafted in full by the analysis team and submitted for restyling or rewriting to the highest authority representing the user. It should be addressed to the next lower level of user management. These managers must be personally briefed and interviewed before any of their subordinates are involved.

3. *Prepare tentative first-pass plan.* Prepare a tentative plan and schedule for first-pass interviews and meetings with user personnel. These plans should be prepared so that they can be reviewed and completed during the management interviews.

4. *Schedule and conduct management interviews.* Allow time to juggle schedules and make appointments. The purpose of these interviews is to brief management on the purpose and approach to system analysis and to establish the gross functions to be analyzed, considered for automation, revised, or ignored. This is also a good time to get cross opinions (to be kept in confidence) on other managers' methods and problems.

The preliminary operational concept document should be as complete as possible at this time, emphasizing the following items:

- A one-paragraph brief on how each function is presently performed
- A description of all outputs provided by the present system
- A description of all additional outputs desired from a new system
- An indication of the desirable features of the present system
- An indication of problems or undesirable features of the present system
- Reasonable/ideal desires under a new system
- Required interface to other functions
- A list of subfunctions with a sentence on each
- The names of user personnel associated with each function/subfunction who should be contacted to gain entire picture
- A candid opinion (in confidence) on the performance of other managers' functions and how these might be improved

5. *Obtain and review applicable literature:* Obtain any documentation on the application and corresponding procedures used; review carefully.

6. *Organize functional outline:* Review and compare notes defining major functions and subfunctions and refine/rewrite outline accordingly. Look for multiply-used subfunctions. List questions to be answered under each function/subfunction.

7. *Circulate documentation:* Return the preliminary operational concept document to the managers who were interviewed for their comments; maintain document for future reference.

8. *Finalize first-pass plan:* Finalize the plan and overall schedules for the first pass with user management.

## 5.4 FIRST PASS

The first pass is the period during which the bulk of information required to permit system analysis is extracted. The preliminary operational concept document should be completed, as should the general requirements document.

If the initialization was performed properly, the interviewing analysts should have a good outline of the functions and subfunctions to be analyzed. Preparation and organization cannot be stressed enough because they are what affords a smooth relation between analysts and user personnel and the resulting passage of information. They also allow the analysis of fairly large systems in two major passes, provided the information is available.

During the first pass, the following functions should be performed:

1. *Schedule Appointments.* Allow a reasonable amount of time to

juggle schedules, review data collected, and prepare for next meeting. Allow for multiple meetings with key people or groups of people where necessary.

2. *Prepare written interview outline.* Prepare written outlines for each interview, leaving enough space after questions to fill in answers. Prepare statements, definitions, and descriptions to be reviewed and clarified where applicable.

3. *Conduct interviews and meetings.* To assure that interviews are well planned and straight to the point, minimize actual meeting time. Two hours per meeting is generally a maximum for user concentration.

4. *Document interview information.* Document all information received during each interview and organize it into a series of memorandum reports so that decisions can be referenced back to user interviews for support.

5. *Organize functional information.* Organize the functional part of the general requirements document into the form of a user's manual and necessary interface specifications (refer to Chapter 6). It may be helpful to rough out a system overview at this point, keeping in mind that this can change drastically, depending on the application.

6. *Prepare documentation.* Complete the preliminary operational concept document and the general requirements document. In addition, a preliminary documentation set should be put together in skeletal form at this point. Time should also be taken to put together an initial user's manual.

7. *Submit functional information for review.* Submit the initial written material describing the system functional requirements for review by user representatives.

## 5.5 SECOND PASS

The second pass is the period during which all remaining information rquired to completely specify the system functional requirements is collected. If the first pass was properly documented, user representatives should quickly identify those areas that are not clearly specified. During the second pass, emphasis should be on confirmation of written descriptions as opposed to verbal interviews and note taking.

The following functions should be performed during the second pass:

1. *Schedule initial management review.* Solicit a review with top user management of the written material submitted at the end of the first pass. Schedule this review based on comments regarding initial documents and supporting material submitted. Allow enough time to ensure that the "top-down" view of the functional description is well understood and accepted.

2. *Schedule appointments.* Schedule second pass appointments with

user personnel based on their initial comments, as well as on inputs from the initial management review.

3. *Conduct interviews and meetings.* Organize each interview or meeting around the clarification of a written document to specify a section of the system functional requirements. The second pass cannot be completed until all of the system functions have been documented in detail, in some form, and agreed on by the user representatives as being complete and correct.

## 5.6 DOCUMENTATION

During the documentation period, a written description of the system functional requirements should be set down in detail. Any written functional description of the system is best put into the framework of the final documentation set (refer to Chapter 6). This is helpful for at least three reasons. First, the system documentation framework should be the best framework for presenting the total final system. Second, if the present documentation standard does not provide the best framework, this should be determined early. Third, continual refinement of the final documentation set appears to be the most practical implementation and enforcement of the "top-down" design approach.

Additional consideration must also be given to the fact that many system specifications are best presented separately from the software system functional description because they represent significant nonstandard items. Examples are existing hardware configuration, memory partition size limitations, communications interface, and so forth. It follows that a suitable method for documentation is to provide an overall skeleton specification document that references the software system documentation set and includes or references hardware and performance-oriented specifications. This can be accomplished with the use of the general requirements document and the documentation set.

To complete the documentation for the functional specification phase, a preliminary operational concept document must be prepared, along with the general requirements document and a major part of the preliminary documentation set. These documents are outlined in Section 5.8 and in the documentation standard (Chapter 6).

Certainly the most difficult documents to develop are the preliminary documentation set. Experience indicates that the best way to develop these documents for software system functional requirements specification is to follow the steps prescribed below. As with any such attempt, an iterative process necessarily will be superimposed in practice.

1. *Output formats. A software system is defined primarily by the outputs it provides to its users.* Anyone who has been involved in enough

system developments over their entire lifecycle is well aware of the importance of this statement. At this stage emphasis should be on close resemblance of the display format to actual envisioned output. In addition, consideration must be given to available output device capability so that devised formats fall within the allowed device range. Communication output formats should also be developed now but may be better placed under a separate heading.

2. *Database.* Once the outputs are defined, the next step is to define the database required to produce those outputs. The rule to be followed is that nothing should be contained within the database that is not required to produce output. Consideration also must be given to the method for database organization. Final database organization is generally the most critical design item is in a user-oriented application system. Normally it is arrived at after much iteration through considering required outputs, sources of input, system and access, scheduling of outputs, and so forth. At this point it is doubtful that a final database design can be achieved. However, all of the elements necessary to provide the required outputs should be specified in detail.

3. *Input Formats.* It may be necessary to specify certain input formats while deciding on the organization of the database. At this point in the development cycle, all imputs required to construct and maintain the database should be available and specified in terms of timeliness as well as content. Communication input formats must also be included at this time but may be better placed under a separate heading.

4. *User's manual and system overview.* One of the primary outputs of the functional analysis and specification phase is an initial user's manual describing the system from a user's standpoint. In addition, the system overview should descirbe the overall functional relationships in general terms and can be oriented around hardware if specified. However, a functional flow that is meaningful to the user and the user's technical representatives is important and necessary.

## 5.7 FINALIZATION

If the documentation period has been properly completed, a written description of the functional requirements of the system has been generated by the analysis team, under close guidance from user management and staff. When this functional description is submitted formally to the user, there should be no surprises about the requirements. The finalization period is a time for (1) review of these functional requirements—planning and estimating the time and resources needed for project continuation and completion—and (2) a go-no go decision on continuing to the environment phase. The following steps are offered:

1. *Functional requirements specification.* At this point the user

should be aware of what will be required on his part to preform final review and acceptance of the functional requirements specification. Copies of this document should be formally submitted to the user and a time period allotted based on the following:

- Time required by the user for final review of the specifications
- Time required to refine the project plan based on knowledge accumulated in Phase II.
- Time required to refine estimates of time and resources required to continue and complete the project
- Joint review of plan and decisions

2. *Project plan.* The overall project plan should be revised and refined based on the knowledge obtained from Phase II. A detailed plan for Phase III should be developed.

3. *Time and resource estimation.* Estimates of time and resources required to complete the project should be revised and refined. Phase III estimates should be done in detail.

4. *Joint review.* A final joint review of specifications, plan changes, and TPM cost estimates with user and developer management should mark the end of Phase II. A decision regarding how and when to proceed to Phase III should result from this joint review.

## 5.8 FUNCTIONAL SPECIFICATION DOCUMENT STANDARDS

The process of automating a given system can cause major changes to existing operating policies and procedures, particularly if the subject system involves a high degree of human interaction (for example, data entry and query). Under such circumstances it is critical that certain analysis and design tasks follow standards that are strictly enforced. The approach proposed within the incremental method for enforcing standards is *management's review of the written word.* Accordingly, this appendix outlines a proposed set of documents leading to a functional specification. Emphasis has been placed on ensuring analyst understanding of rationale behind policies and procedures of the present system and on assuring that specification of the proposed system be developed in a manner that is clearly visible to the user and the user's representatives and is couched in terms with which they are familiar.

Developers of hardware can have a distinct advantage over their counterparts in software. When they solicit customers to envision the impact of a new hardware device on its proposed environment, the visual nature of hardware is generally clear. New software systems also can have a considerable effect on their environments and can provide substantial improvements over the systems and methods they replace; however, these effects are more difficult to visualize, particularly with applications being automated for the first time. As a result, a clear description of the final product must be maintained for constant user review throughout the development effort. If this is not done, the developer encourages the risk of presenting an undesirable final product that, although formally accepted, may never be used. The documents proposed here are intended to bridge the gap between the system as envisioned by the user and that envisioned by the developer.

Three working documents are necessary to the development of a system specification during the functional analysis and specification phase. These are "working" documents in the sense that they are files for design decision rationale, and they should evolve one after the other. They are titled as follows:

1. Preliminary operational concept
2. General requirements
3. Preliminary documentation set

The following sections provide a general description and outline of each of these documents, with comments where appropriate.

## 5.9 PRELIMINARY OPERATIONAL CONCEPT

This document must define the environment of the new system in terms of the methodology and doctrine of the existing system, which may be manual. Its cooperative preparation should assist both the user and the developer in learning how the application best can be automated. Users must be encouraged to focus on what they are to get in relation to what they have. The risk of divergence of user requirements can thereby be reduced. The system developer benefits by having a written reference to user doctrine during the design/development phases to ensure that unanticipated requirements are included in the evolving implementation. The document is outlined as follows:

1. Description of policy and procedures currently utilized
   a. Description of the organization where the procedures and doctrines are employed—including size, geographic location, and logical organization
   b. How policies and procedures are invoked and performed; by whom; number of personnel evolved
   c. Cost/performance trade-off of the new system in terms of manpower saved or other advantages expected
2. Overall description of the desired system
   a. Functional block diagram for each configuration

b. Identification of users and operators from organizational point of view, giving numbers of users and operators
c. Identification of system capabilities by user type
(1) General outputs required and from where initiated
(2) Inputs available: where, when, how, and from whom
(3) Chain of review of inputs and outputs
d. Utilization of the system from an operator's viewpoint
e. System backup
f. System security
3. Relationship of old procedures to desired system
a. Areas of direct commonality
b. Areas of deviation and anticipated effects of the new system on user procedures
4. Overall description of how the system interacts operationally with other systems
a. Operational procedures to be automated that will impact other systems
b. Relationship of the system's operational procedures and policies to the other systems' operational procedures and policies

## 5.10 GENERAL REQUIREMENTS

This document is divided into three parts; functional requirements, performance requirements, and environment requirements. In essence, the document must provide the detail on what the system must do, how fast this should be done, and under what environmental (user functional) restrictions. Much of the information in this document will evolve from the preliminary operational concept. The document is outlined as follows:

1. Functional requirements
a. Top-down breakout of the system functions (modes)
(1) Delineation of the topmost breakout of the system functions (modes), if possible including a rationale, from the user's viewpoint, for the breakout. (Note: Functional breakout may *not* correspond to a software system physical breakout, which can evolve later
(2) If the system will have more than one configuration, provision of a functional breakout for each configuration
b. Inclusion of the following for each function
(1) General description of the functional requirements
(2) Function initiation and termination and relationship of each mode to the total system/function
(3) Functional outputs and their relationship to operational needs

(4) Source of functional inputs and their relationship to available operational data
(5) Interaction with the operator
(6) Relationship of the function to other functions

c. System backup
(1) Relationship to operational need
(2) How implemented by functional breakout

d. System security
(1) Relationship to operational need
(2) How implemented by functional breakout

2. Performance requirements
a. Current system performance statistics and discussion
(1) Throughput
(2) Response times by function

b. New system's desired performance statistics
(1) Assumptions
(2) Throughput
(3) Response times by function

c. Human factors performance considerations
(1) Allowed error rates
(2) Time to enter data or respond

3. Application environment requirements
a. System physical requirements
(1) Location
(2) Transportability
(3) Size
(4) Weight
(5) Power

b. Maintenance requirements
(1) Maintenance philosophy
(2) System logistics (where software will be maintained over its lifecycle)

c. Reliability requirements
(1) System MTBF (mean time between failures)
(2) System MTTR (mean time to restart)

d. Hardware restrictions
(1) Standard subsystem or component restrictions
(2) Standard interface restrictions

4. Development environment requirements
a. Software environment restrictions/philosophy/tools
(1) Off-line and on-line support systems
(2) Languages
(3) Support operating systems
(4) Library facilities
(5) Linkage philosophy

(6) Testing tools
(7) System generation
(8) Documentation tools
(9) Management tools

b. Hardware environment restrictions
(1) Location
(2) Maintenance
(3) Reliability
(4) Availability
(5) Specific equipment restrictions

## 5.11 PRELIMINARY DOCUMENTATION SET

The preliminary documentation set must contain preliminary versions of the following items from the external documentation set:

- User's manual
- Operator's manual
- System overview
- Human interface specification
- Database specification
- Communications interface specification

These documents (described in Chapter 6) are considered preliminary in the sense that they may not follow precisely the standard format, may not be used, and may contain some rationale supporting design decisions. They should be complete enough, however, to provide the foundation upon which to build a detailed design and final external documentation set.

If properly prepared, the preliminary user's manual is probably the most difficult document to develop. It is also the most important in that it must spell out all policies and procedures to be used in the new system. It must be a clear presentation of the final system as seen by the user.

# CHAPTER 6

# Documentation

## 6.1 INTRODUCTION

Documentation is the essential element for defining user-oriented software systems and providing independence from the original authors. A major source of software problems arises when users associate "comments in the code" with documentation. *Software documentation*, as used in this book, derives its meaning from the structure and definition of the software product as defined in Section 1.8. The *documentation standards* defined in this chapter cover the *external documentation library* defined within the software product. This dichotomy is essential to the software design process that is embodied in evolving the layers of detail that make up the external documentation library. The software documentation standards offered here provide a framework to support a highly structured approach to the design, construction, support, and use of a software product over its lifecycle.

The purpose of a documentation standard is to aid software developers in providing clear and concise descriptions of the system and of individual programs as they relate to the end user, operating personnel, and persons who must technically support the system. In particular, a documentation standard should be aimed at producing the following attributes in a documentation library:

- Providing a clear understanding between user and developer about what the system will do *before detailed software design*
- Providing a clear understanding between designers and programmers about what the program modules will do *before coding*
- Allowing the end user to initiate requests and interpret outputs without the aid of a computer technician
- Allowing operators to execute instruction from the end user without the aid of an analyst or programmer
- Allowing the system to be supported or enhanced independent of the original authors
- Allowing other programs or systems to be integrated without assistance from the original authors

It is important to observe that software development support typically requires that a large portion of man-hours be spent clarifying how processes are invoked, how they work, and how they interact with other processes in the system. Experience has demonstrated that understanding can be gained most quickly by reading well-structured documents in *plain English*, annotated with good diagrams and tables. Nothing is more time consuming and frustrating than trying to derive such information from program listings. Program listings cannot be organized in a hierarchical structure and don't lend themselves to descriptive writing that can be supplemented with pictures. Internal program documentation should be limited to comments that explain unreadable source code and change history. All higher level documentation must reside in the external documentation library.

## 6.2 BACKGROUND RATIONALE

The documentation library for a particular application must be self-contained to the maximum extent possible. It should not refer to other documentation except when disjoint from the application. In particular, it should contain the detailed description of the entire database that it references.

Because this standard is concerned with large user-oriented systems and because these generally are database oriented, it is convenient to organize the documentation with direct access to the database. In many cases, it is similarly convenient to have direct access to human readable output formats, communications formats, and input formats, so this material also must be provided. Incorporating these items into separate documents within an overall library results in the following advantages:

- The assigning of identical common names and descriptions within each program to all external program references
- The elimination of redundant descriptions of identical data from individual program documentation via a symbolic file/record reference system or a similar heirarchical structure
- Ease of considering any changes to the database structure in light of how they affect the total system
- The availability of a simple procedure for ensuring that any database changes are properly reflected throughout the system
- Availability of the complete database description in one condensed document for handy reference

For the purpose of instructing and guiding the user, or as an aid to gaining a clear understanding of the system, it is generally convenient to break the software into functional parts. In many software systems, particularly interactive systems in which the user is on-line to the database, the software functional structure is very different from the functional structure that a user sees. For example, in a word processing system, the user may want to insert text into an existing paragraph. The user's manual would describe the *insert* function from a user's standpoint. The structure of the software functions that must be implemented to perform the insert function (for example, reading the keyboard, controlling the screen, updating the data files) bears little resemblance to the structure of the insert function the user perceives.

When designing or supporting software, one must be able to translate easily from user functions to software functions, particularly when tracing problems. A convenient rule to establish for fault isolation is that a subprogram will not span (perform) more than one major software function. In fact, many subprograms may be used to perform one software function. In these cases it will be convenient to break each function into subfunctions that correspond to subprograms or groups of subprograms.

When subprograms are used in more than one subfunction, they will be termed *utility* programs and combined under a separate *utilities* section. In such cases the subfunction can be defined by specifying its external references to the corresponding utility and by referring to the utility subfunction for further detail.

## 6.3 EXTERNAL DOCUMENTATION OUTLINE

The following items make up the external documentation library. Brief explanations accompany each (refer to Figure 6.1).

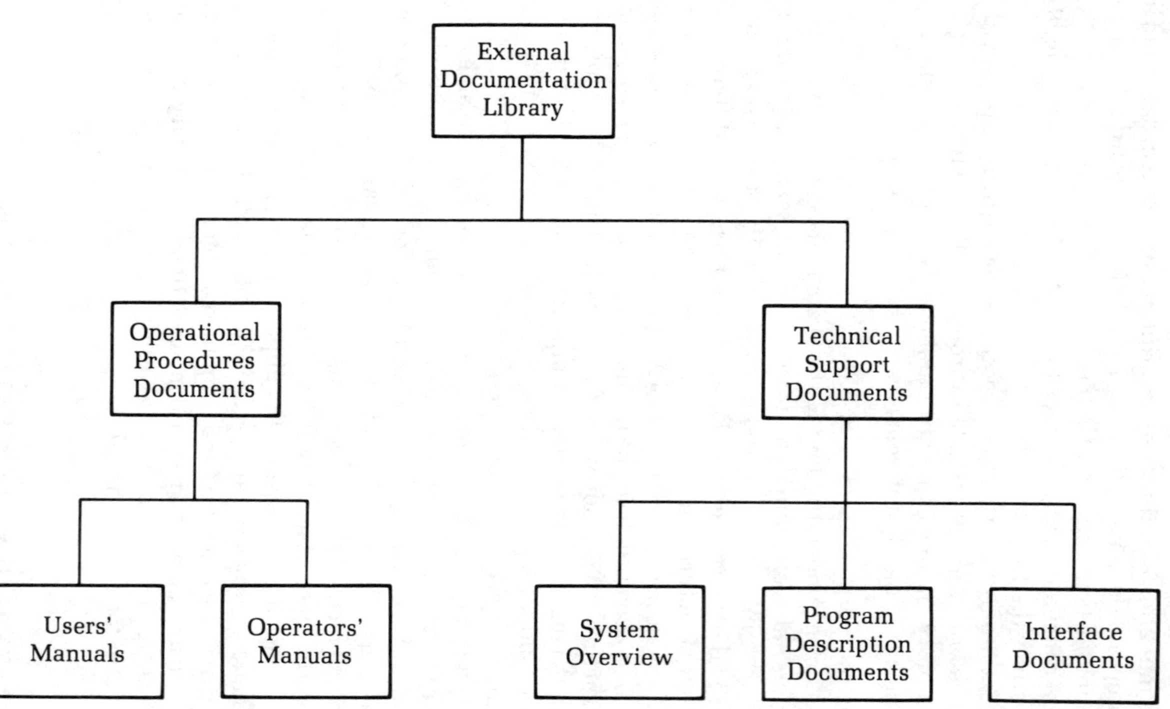


**Figure 6.1a.** External Documentation Library.

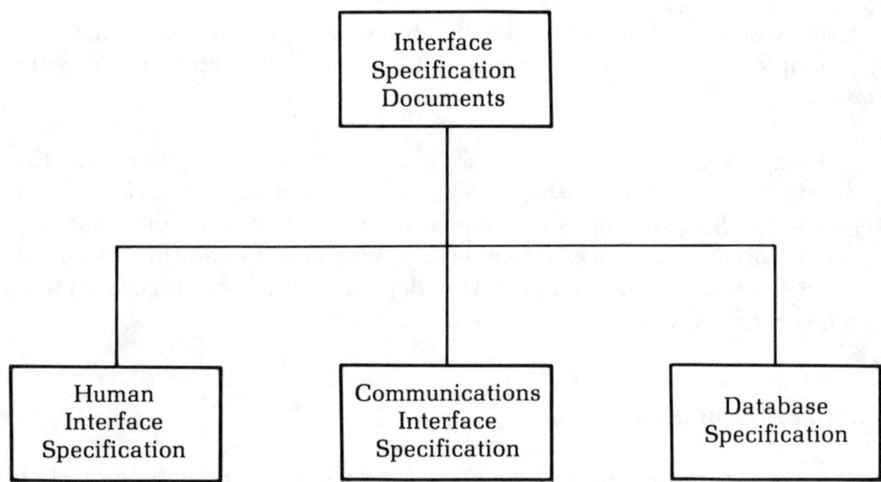


**Figure 6.1b.** External Documentation Library.

## Operating Procedures Documents

*User's Manual.* This is the most important item in the documentation set. it completely defines the system from a user functional standpoint, with the aid of the human interface document. It should provide sufficient instruction so that the user can use (or direct operators to use) the system and interpret output without the aid of a computer technician.

*Operating Procedures Manual.* This manual should instruct the operator on the interpretation of directions from the user and should describe the corresponding procedures to be followed so that operations can be performed without assistance from an analyst or programmer. In some applications the end user and operator may be the same person, in which case the user and operating manuals can be combined.

## Technical Support Documents

*System Overview.* This document provides the road map to all of the software functions in the system. The overview can be accomplished using software functional block diagrams, modified HIPO* diagrams, and brief narrative descriptions of all of the software functions in the system.

*HIPO (Hierarchical Input Processing Output) is a trademark of IBM.

These are described in Section 6.6. When the user functional specifications are complete, the system overview can be used as the top-level software design document.

*Program Descriptions.* These must contain descriptions of the individual subsystems, with corresponding programs in sufficient detail to allow modification or enhancement of the system without assistance from the original authors. These descriptions also contain the details of each utility used in the system and the details of standard procedures that are incorporated into more than one subfunction.

### Interface Documents

*Human Interface Specifications.* This document depicts the visible output and input formats in a form that should closely resemble the display format, or provide a good visual likeness. It should contain a sample for each format, with references to specify display formats or provide all display information directly on the sample.

*Database Specifications.* This document describes all internal (intraprogram) and external (interprogram) databases in a hierarchical structure.

*Communications Interface Specifications.* This document describes the communication protocols—that is, the form in which the applications programs must present information to the communications system.

## 6.4 MANAGEMENT PLANNING AND MILESTONES

Documentation should start at the earliest possible stages in the development cycle (Phase II in the incremental method) and be formally completed, except for the most detailed internal program module descriptions, *before coding* unless subsystems can be completed and tested on an independent basis. The first item to be completed will be the user's manual, which should be reviewed and approved by the user before other dependent parts of the documentation are finalized. Generally, all other items in the documentation library may be worked on concurrently. Any documents referenced in the user's manual, however, should be finalized along with that manual.

The level of effort required to complete the user's manual will depend on the following:

- Degree of complexity of the system

- Effectiveness of the analysis phase and quality of the resulting documentation
- Automation experience existing for the application
- User's level of understanding of functional requirements and user's ability to organize and communicate them

A chart of documentation milestones is shown in Figure 6.2. It is organized with respect to the phases within the incremental method. The chart is not intended to be used for precise time scaling. Rather, it should be used as a guide for the following points:

1. The individual items should start to take shape as documents at the approximate position of the tail of the arrow.
2. All items should be brought to a final-form version before the end of certain phases, as indicated by the large circles. In particular, the operating procedures manual and the system overview and interface documents must be in final form before the end of Phase III. These are the "design to" documents for Phase IV; they will be referred to as the preliminary documentation set. The subsystem descriptions must be completed before the end of Phase IV. Thus a complete final version of the external documentation is prepared before initiation of the program (source code) development, Phase V.
3. All items should be finalized before the end of the phase containing the head of the arrow. From the finalized version of each documentation item forward (point 2 above), originals and a working copy should be kept under tight control. All revisions must then proceed in accordance with strict revision processes as described in Chapter 9.

## 6.5 PROCEDURES MANUALS

The procedures manuals, together with the human interface document, must explain the use and operation of the system in clear terms without need for assistance from analysts, programmers, or original authors. In some systems the "user" functions will be separate from the "operator" functions and must be split into separate manuals. In other systems these functions may be combined, and a single manual will suffice.

### User's Manual

The user's manual must completely define the system from a user functional standpoint, with the aid of the human interface document. It

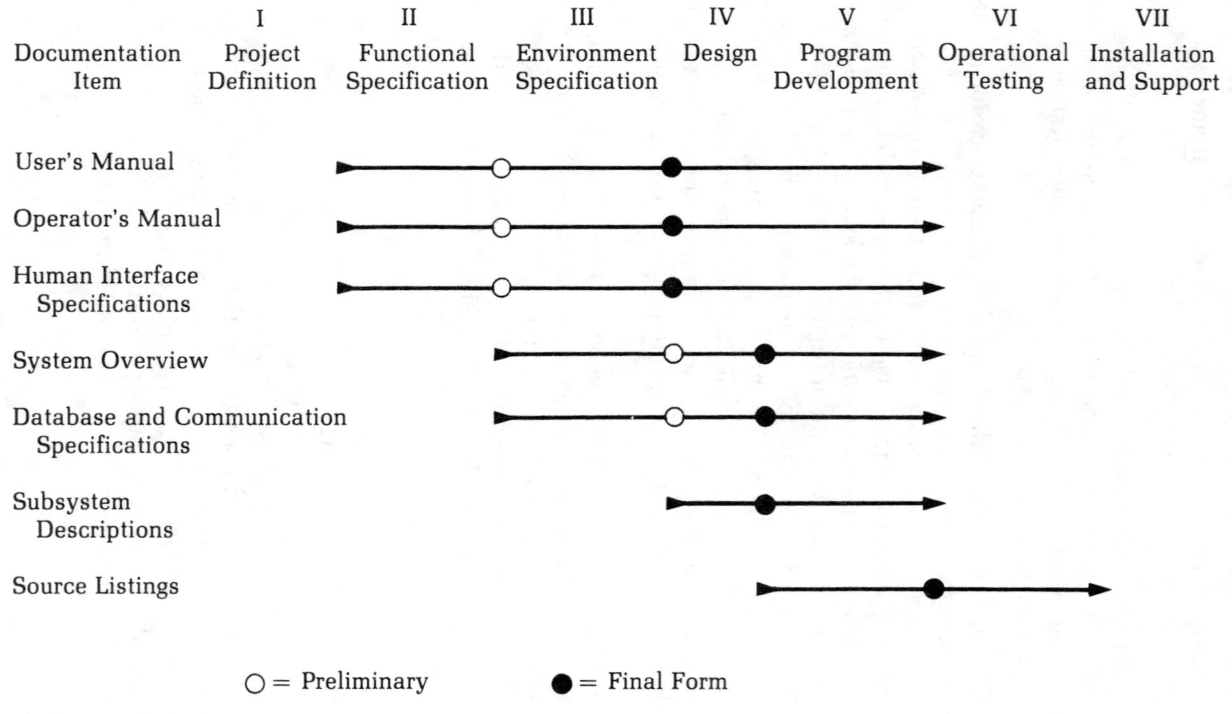


**Figure 6.2.** Documentation Phases.

should provide sufficient instruction so that the end user can direct operators to query and update the system as well as interpret output without the aid of a computer technician.

The User's Manual can contain instructions that deal with functions other than those directly controlled by software. Often this can be done to provide a convenient reference within one manual. The willingness of the user to accept a system and utilize it on a long-term basis will depend heavily on how well this manual is written.

*Organization.* The user's manual should be organized functionally into contiguous steps as would be performed under normal operation. It should start with an overview of the system and should describe its basic approach and philosophies where applicable. Sections concerned with editing and validating inputs should come first, followed by construction and control of the database. A separate section describing the organization of the database from a user's point of view may be desirable. Query and report facilities should come next, followed by utilities and standard procedures. If the sections and subsections of this manual can be labeled according to the standard numbering system that holds throughout the documentation, this will greatly aid the user to communicate with operators and support personnel.

*Contents.* The contents of each function and subfunction section should follow a pattern if possible, with the following items contained under each section when applicable.

1. *Input information.* The user must be told precisely what input information he must provide, and in what format, to properly execute a system function. If input is edited by the system, the user should be told what edit and validation checks are performed and the data limitations that exist. The user should be provided with sample display depicting how he would have to prepare or view the edit and validation checks. It may be possible to reference the human interface document for this purpose.

2. *Control options.* Any options available to the user and their controls should be fully explained.

3. *Scheduling.* If frequency of operation or deadlines are applicable to a given function, they should be explained.

4. *System resource estimates.* If an estimation of utilization of system resources is required, this should be explained so that the user can make the estimates and pass control to the operator.

5. *Monitor information.* If information can be provided so that the user can alert the operator early regarding possible malfunctions, the manual should provide these hints. Timing estimates and key output words can be helpful here.

6. *Interpretation of output.* Interpretation of output should be clearly specified through the use of sample displays or reports. The use of reference numbers next to circled data samples that are explained on a separate sheet are helpful. The human interface document can also be used as a reference. All anticipated error or exception conditions should be fully explained.

7. *Disposition of output.* Routing or disposing of communications output or hard copy should be specific where applicable.

8. *Recovery.* If recovery procedures have been developed for certain possible malfunctions, these should be explained to the extent required for the user's understanding.

## Operator's Manual

The operating procedures manual should provide sufficient direction for the operator to execute user instructions without any programming knowledge or assistance.

*Organization.* The operating procedures manual should be organized functionally into the same contiguous steps as is the user's manual. The use of a standard numbering system will greatly assist the operator in communicating with user and support personnel. Because an operator is dealing with the same set of devices to perform each function or subfunction, organizing instructions onto standard forms can be convenient. If this application is one of a number being performed at a given site, standard forms already may be available or imposed. If the hardware system to be used exists in other previously developed applications, one should investigate their forms and take advantage of refinements learned from experience. Independent of how input data and instructions are passed to the operator, it is desirable to reduce operator directions to a set of standard forms that can be interpreted for each function to be performed. Normally these would be covered in the operations standard at a given installation.

*Contents.* The contents of each function or subfunction section should follow a pattern if possible. If standard forms are used, they will impose a pattern that operators will learn. The following items should be explained where applicable.

1. Function/subfunction description
   Designation
   Organization control
   Classification
   Priority

2. *Scheduling*
   Timing
   Frequency
   Duration
3. *Resource requirements*
   Software
   Devices/units/channels
   Modes/volume
   Forms/alignment
4. *Inputs*
   Source
   Description
   Format
   Volume
5. *Initialization procedures*
   Storage media
   Forms
   Recording of starting data
6. *Monitor instructions*
   Alert conditions
   Messages
   Errors/exceptions
7. *Termination procedures*
   Normal termination
   Recovery
   Restart
   Abort
   Recording of termination data
8. *Outputs*
   Source
   Description
   Interpretation
   Volume
   Disposition
9. *Special instructions*
   Anything not covered conveniently elsewhere
   Anything requiring special attention

## 6.6 TECHNICAL SUPPORT DOCUMENTS

The technical support documents, in conjunction with the procedures documents, interface documents, and source listings, must allow the system to be maintained or enhanced without the aid of the original authors. They should also allow other programs or systems to be integrated independently. These documents assume that the reader has sufficient programming knowledge to understand standard techniques and terminology easily referenced elsewhere. Special techniques or terminology peculiar to this application or a small class of applications should be explained. Borderline cases should be referenced if not explained.

## System Overview

The system overview provides a technical as well as software functional overview of the system. It should be initiated early in Phase III along with the environment specifications.

*Organization.* The system overview should be organized around software functions that correspond to the physical software design, starting with an overview of the entire system. At its most detailed layer, this document must identify the bottom-level software modules. Actual descriptions of these modules would be contained in the program description document. Figure 6.3 provides a pictorial representation of a typical "software system tree."

A convenient method for organizing structured descriptions of software is shown in Figure 6.4, which depicts a software function block

**Figure 6.3.** The Software System Tree.

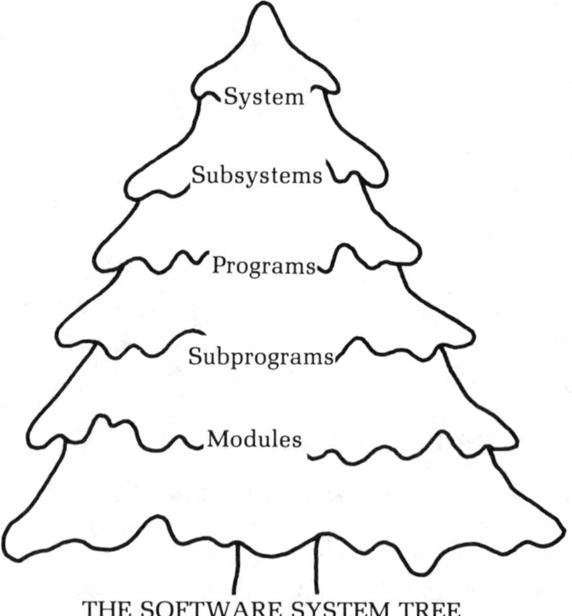

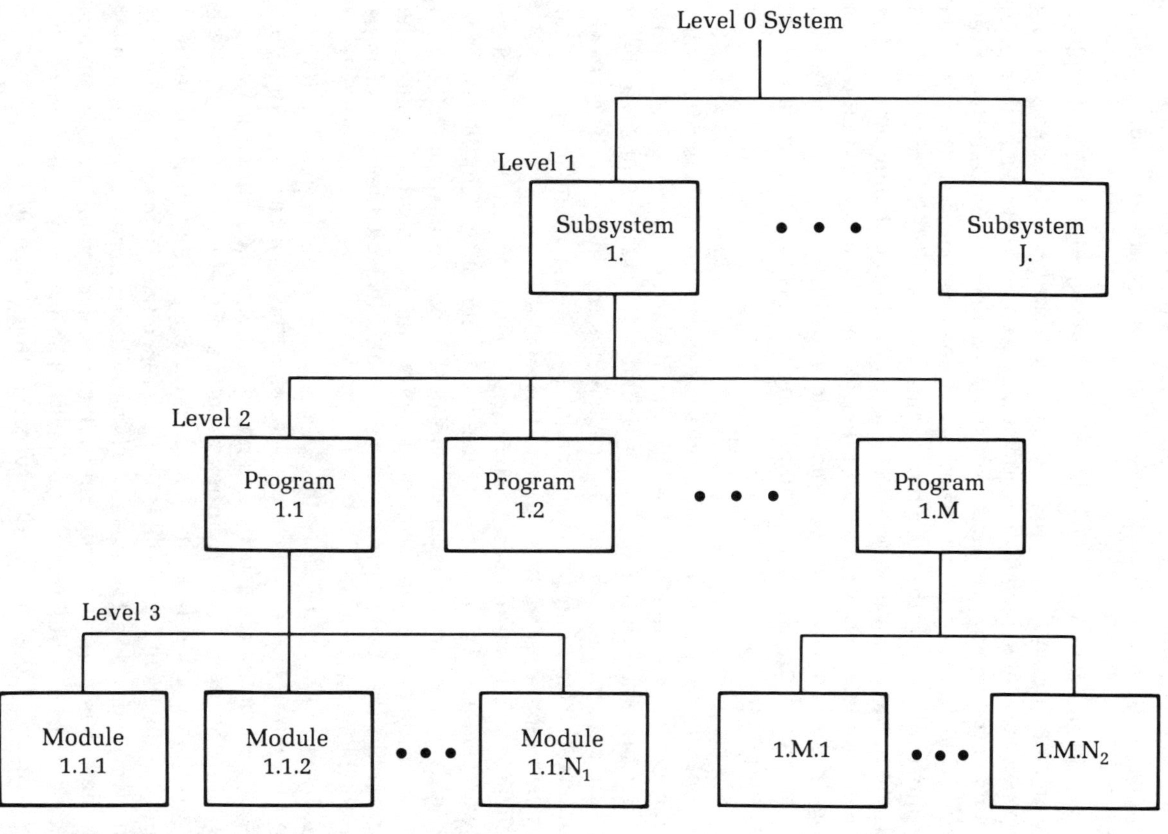


**Figure 6.4.** Software Function Block Diagram.

diagram. The purpose of this diagram is to show the hierarchical relationship of physical software elements that make up the system. It is important to understand that the software functional boxes typically bear little or no resemblance to the system functions from a user standpoint. For example, bottom-level modules typically will be utilities, such as file handlers.

The organization of the system overview should follow the block diagram, starting at the top (level 0), which describes the system as being comprised of subsystems. The document would then be broken into sections corresponding to these subsystems. Each subsystem would be described in terms of its programs, with corresponding sections broken into subsections describing each program. This type of breakdown would continue to the level just above the bottom module. The number of levels needed would depend on the size of the system. The numbers in the boxes in Figure 6.4 can correspond to the table of contents of the document, as well as provide a hierarchical numbering scheme for the software functions and modules.

*Content.* Starting at level 0 with a description of the system, each section should contain a software functional block diagram, a HIPO, and a brief narrative description of that particular software element. Note that a software element as defined here corresponds to a block on the software functional block diagram. The modules at the bottom level are not described separately, only as part of the level above.

The block diagram need only cover two levels for any particular software element. For example, when describing the system (level 0), one need only show the top level system block and the next level (level 1) subsystem blocks. When describing a program, one need only show the program block and the corresponding module blocks. Other levels can be described similarly.

The HIPO should follow the form shown in Figure 6.5. Inputs and outputs contain entries that must reference the data-base specification. This is best accomplished by assigning a unique code to each file and record in the data base. Additional details are given in the data-base specification section later in this chapter. Each entry in the input and output section contains a data-base reference that is shared between at least two modules in the system. These will be interprogram databases (external files) or intraprogram databases (common areas of main memory shared by an executable task). The processing portion of the HIPO contains the names of processes that make up the particular software element being described. In a large system convenient to assign a unique code to each of these processes. Many of these processes will be utilities that will be used in at least two different HIPOs.

The brief narrative should contain enough information to help the reader understand the organization of the system, subsystem, program,

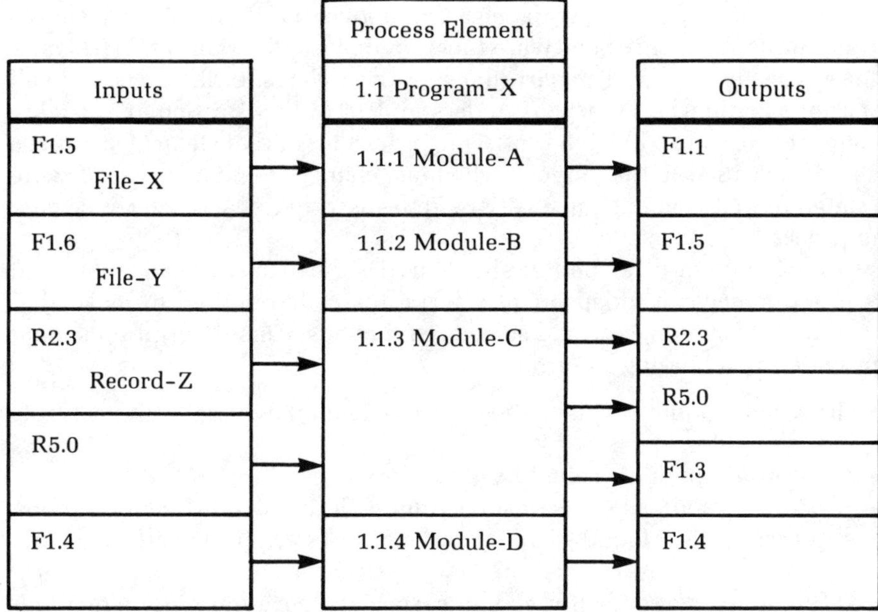


**Figure 6.5.** Heirarchical Input Process Out (HIPO) Diagram.

and so forth. The narrative should not go into the functional properties of the system from a software standpoint, other than those that can be helpful as a road map. It should contain information that helps relate how the user functions are implemented in the software. Thus system overview provides a road map from user functions to software functions.

### Program Descriptions

The program descriptions provide the detailed descriptions of each subsystem, program, and corresponding bottom-level modules. They must bridge the gap between the procedures manuals and the source listings to provide a clear understanding of the details of each software module in the system.

*Organization.* The program descriptions document should follow the same organization as the system overview, except that it should contain a separate section for each bottom-level module. Whereas the system overview ends one level above the bottom modules, the major part of the program descriptions is the detailed module descriptions. Therefore, within each program description section there must be a subsection corresponding to each program module contained in that program.

*Content.* Each software element *above* the module level should contain the same set of software functional block diagrams and HIPOs as the system overview. The narratives for these elements should contain all the information necessary to understand how that particular software element is organized. All the software properties of that element should be clearly specified so that anyone who must change or enhance the software related to that element can easily read the description and determine how to proceed.

Each bottom-level module should be described in enough detail so that a programmer can independently write the code required to make that module perform its expected software functions. This description should provide the following information:

- How this module is called and controlled and how it calls and controls other modules
- A list of all modules called by this module
- For utility modules (those called from at least two different software elements), a list of all the calling modules to determine the effects of any changes
- Difficult areas of code (for example, special algorithms or data manipulation processes)
- Modifications to shared databases (for example, common memory areas or files), along with any conditions that affect these changes
- Abort procedures, operator messages, or debug features

If a module is a utility module, then its detailed module description should be contained in the utilities section as described in the following paragraphs. References to a utility from any program in the system need only specify the name and unique code of that utility. The reader then can refer to the common utilities section to obtain the detailed description of that module.

## Utilities

The utilities section contains the detailed descriptions of each utility used in the system. A software element is a utility if it is used by two or more higher level software elements. Note that a utility may be a module or a combination of modules (for example, a program). The program descriptions should not redundantly explain the details of a utility but should emphasize the particular aspects of applying and controlling the utility, and should reference the utilities section for more detail.

If a utility is a "system" utility (that is, a standard program supplied with the system support software) and it is explained elsewhere, then reference may be made directly to the support software documentation as long as it will be as readily available as the system documentation.

*Organization.* The utilities section should be organized in the same manner as the program descriptions, being an extension of them. It should be included at the end of the program descriptions.

*Content.* The content should be the same as for the program descriptions. Particular care must be taken to document utility modules (bottom level) because they may do different things for different calling modules.

## 6.7 INTERFACE SPECIFICATIONS

The interface specifications provide direct access to detailed descriptions of the following: (1) human inputs and outputs, (2) databases, and (3) communications protocols. Because these specifications are referenced by most of the other documentation, it is convenient if a common framework can be used for reference identifiers. For example, a combination of letters and numbers can be used for codes that tell the reader if the specification is part of a database and whether it is a file or a record. Hierarchical numbering schemes can be used to show what program or module originates the records of outputs being referenced. Such a numbering scheme can be derived directly from the software functional block diagram or the HIPO. As an example, *OF*1.4.2-3 can be used to identify the third *O*utput *F*ile created by Module 1.4.2.

The particular indexing scheme used is not nearly as important as having a scheme. In the software design phase many interface specifications will be created and destroyed. Therefore, during this period, it is most helpful if their reference identifiers carry pertinent information. The need for this information is just as important when new personnel are called on to support the system after the original authors have departed. The interface specifications are described in the succeeding sections.

### Human Interface Specifications

*Output Formats.* The output formats contain descriptions of all of the outputs visible to a human. These should be depicted in a form that is as close as possible to the actual display or print format. Complete detail must be provided on all display options so that devices or forms can be specified, and the programs coded. It is helpful to tag each field on a display output specification whose meaning is not obvious. These tags then can provide an index on a separate sheet, with explanations of each corresponding field. Because it is convenient to reference the output formats from the users manual, they should be explained in a manner the user can understand.

*Input Formats.* The input formats must depict the visible input formats in a manner that closely resembles the display format or provides a good visual likeness. Because the input formats are likely to be referenced from the users manual, they should be presented in manner the user can understand. Explanations should include descriptions of all the fields for insertion, allowed codes and their translations, and any editing that is to be performed automatically.

Many times the human interface specifications can be described using standard forms. Doing this can be helpful in that much of the specification is contained on the form itself and needs to be understood only once.

## Database Specifications

Before we describe the database specification, it must be noted that we are not describing a database management system. We are merely describing the means for documenting a database. By database we mean all of the data shared by two or more modules or programs. This includes external files shared by separate executable tasks and common memory areas shared by modules within a single task. Both can be described in a common data record format.

The main purpose of the database specification is to provide all information required to properly access, utilize, and update the database with programs or modules other than those originating it. This document must provide the common specification of data that is shared by different processes in the system. Changes to this specification must be carefully controlled, because they must be compatible with all modules sharing the changed data.

Elements of the database can be viewed in a hierarchical structure, starting with bits, characters, and fields. Fields may take on the special property of being keys, in which case they are used by processing programs to search, sort, and merge information. However, one can dispense with this special consideration and think of all fields as keys, a more human-oriented approach. Fields can then be grouped into records. In fact, the basic data description element most commonly used is the data record. Records can then be grouped into blocks and blocks into files.

It is convenient to record descriptions of data in two ways simultaneously: (1) a file or record format description and (2) a data element dictionary. Both are described in the following paragraphs.

*File-Record Format Descriptions.* The purpose of the file-record format descriptions is to define file and record layouts in a simple, concise way. A common and convenient approach is to list all fields in the order they occur in the record. The list should include the field mnemonic, field name, field type and length, and the starting character position of the field.

Files can be described in terms of the records they contain, along with any special information (for example, format, maximum record size, and so forth). In the case of internal data records—that is, common areas of main memory that are shared—the same record format descriptions can easily apply to each.

*Data Element Dictionary.* This dictionary is an alphabetical listing of each element in the database, with its corresponding definition. The definitions should be simple to understand and user oriented, because the data element dictionary can be helpful to a user as well as a software technician. The dictionary should be used to define internal memory data areas as well as external files.

### Communications Interface Specifications

The communications interface specifications must describe all of the communications protocols that directly interface any of the software in the system. These descriptions must be sufficiently complete to allow integration with other systems. If descriptions of communications protocols are adequately explained in other documentation that is readily available, then these documents can be referenced. This is an area in which reduncancy should *not* be avoided.

An existing framework for describing communications protocols has evolved over many years of practical implementation in the field of international communications. The framework provides the basis for describing individual protocol standards and the manner in which various protocol standards interrelate. This framework, known as the Reference Model for Open Systems Interconnection (OSI/TC97/SC16), is promulgated by the International Standardization Organization (ISO). The approach taken is to address each layer as a separate and independent protocol layer, starting with the application or presentation (human interface) layer and working to the physical media layer. This approach has provided a framework for easily specifying what heretofore was a difficult problem to describe. Anyone building software for the international market is well advised to contact ISO to obtain a description of the Reference Model for OSI.

## 6.8 REVISION PROCESS

As each documentation item is completed at the solid black circle on the milestone chart (Figure 6.1), it should be put under a rigid revision control process. It is important that all changes be strictly controlled and recorded as a permanent record. This is absolutely necessary when large volumes of documentation are distributed to the customer base as well as to support personnel. Pages can then be replaced individually when updating is done. The control process also provides the means for checking the congruence of outstanding copies with the latest version (For a detailed explanation of the software revision process, including documentation, refer to Chapter 9).

## 6.9 SOURCE LISTINGS

The internal program documentation (source listing) is as important as the external documentation just described—particularly when maintaining or improving the system. Generally, the source code should be clearly structured functionally. Depending on the source language used, the extensive use of notes (in English) may be necessary.

Well-documented FORTRAN code usually requires a minimum of 50% comment statements. Many other languages require a substantially higher ratio of comments to code for readability. COBOL, properly used, requires little need for program comment because the language itself provides the structure and facilities for writing highly readable code. For details on how to write well-documented (easy-to-read and understand) source code, refer to Chapter 7.

# CHAPTER 7

# Programming Standards

## 7.1 BACKGROUND

All of the foregoing management methods for project definition, estimation, design, and documentation are precursors to the task of writing the code or programs. Therefore it is imperative that the same attention be given to programming standards and practices as was given to the previous development phases. Programming standards typically follow lines prescribed by Ledgard and Cave (1976). Specific choices, of course, depend on the particular characteristics of the programming language being used and the requirements of the project under consideration.

Recent experience has demonstrated that the economics of development, integration, and, particularly, the support of software is enhanced by using certain new approaches to writing code. These new approaches include top-down programming, structured programming, and GO TO-less programming. After one has used these new approaches sufficiently, their usefulness becomes obvious. In addition, the resulting standards are easily enforced.

Considering the acclaimed impact that programming languages can have on the economics of software development and support, relatively little has been done to scientifically measure the effects of one language versus another on the software lifecycle cost curve, (Figure 1.1). We have located only two papers that deal directly with productivity as a function of language (Fitzsimmons and Love, 1978; Ledgard et al., 1980). The conclusion is not surprising: Productivity is highest when the language is closest to English. What is surprising is that COBOL, which was designed to be an English-like language, was not considered in any of the comparisons.

Literally hundreds of programming languages exist today, each emphasizing certain types of capabilities, features, or applications. Software vogues are constantly changing, with some languages at times appearing to enjoy higher popularity than others. Languages such as BASIC, Pascal, and "C" are currently popular in the microprocessor field. However, published statistics show that the majority of software for production usage is written in COBOL, with FORTRAN used second most. Both languages have been around for a long time and therefore carry longevity. So, too, have ALGOL and PL/1.

We acknowledge the many other languages that exist and the theoretical reasons why they should be in the number-one spot. Certainly they will be used if they are good. However, as we stated in the Preface, we are addressing only those methods and techniques that have proved themselves in the competitive software product market environment. Therefore we limit our discussions to COBOL and FORTRAN.

On the positive side, neither of these two languages is standing still. COBOL enjoys the National Bureau of Standards' acknowledgement as the only language that provides the basis for complete standardization and portability. This is because in COBOL, all data is specified in terms of number of characters or digits. FORTRAN 77 provides many of the features desired for structured programming, and it has extensive support facilities for scientific calculations. FORTRAN is used as the base language for many special-purpose languages because of its natural expression of algebraic relations. Both FORTRAN and COBOL enjoy the strong support of standardization efforts that are prerequisites to their use for a major software product to be rehostable.

## 7.2 OVERVIEW

The standardization approaches presented here contain principles that at first may appear controversial because they rule out the use of many "sacred" concepts used in programming. These principles are:

1. The readability of programs is the most important programming factor affecting the economics of the lifecycle cost curve (Figure 1.1), particularly the cost of long-term support.
2. The transportability of software from one machine to another makes it much more valuable.

Although it is clear that writing quality programs requires more effort and deeper thought, the overall economics will repay the practitioner.

The thrust of this chapter is to suggest guidelines for good programming practice as well as rigorous standards for writing quality programs. Developing rigorous programming standards is not easy, for the rules should be unambiguous, of sufficient merit so that a programmer will not be unduly stifled by their adoption, and, ideally, machine testable.

The importance of developing such standards is clear. There is great value in adherence to uniform rules so that programmers may more easily read and understand programs written by others. There is a need to use coding techniques that reduce the complexity of programs and ensure portability from one machine to another. There is the need to control the entire programming effort. Ultimately, program standards should be automatically aided and enforced.

No standard can attempt to cover the particular aspects or operating environment of a given programming project. In fact, many features are ruled out to remove ambiguity and ensure transportability and supportability. For those issues not covered, one must trust that a wise programmer will distill the spirit of standardization and apply creativity and good sense to the program at hand.

Finally, no attempt is made to consider the consequences on efficiency. If a particular implementation causes inefficiency in the adoption of standards, then this may be due cause for revocation. However, one of the major roles of a manager during the coding process is maintaining a vigilance against the sacrifice of economic effectiveness for coding efficiencies.

## 7.3 COBOL STANDARDS

The following is a sampling of standards based on the COBOL language.

### General Rules

1. For each installation and project application, there should be a standard set of user-defined words. The rationale here is to develop a well-accepted set of naming conventions and to reduce the time spent by programmers in devising good (but different) names. Having a standard set of words will promote a high degree of readability of programs and will prevent confusion over different names for the same objects. Enforcement of standard names is best accomplished by using the copy library of COBOL to define standard data descriptions and procedures, and the data element dictionary. These can be inserted in programs using the COPY verb. described later in this chapter.

2. Columns 1 through 6 are used for statement sequence numbers, right-adjusted if unfilled. Columns 8 through 72 are used for COBOL statement contents. Columns 73 through 80 are used for system/module identification. Certain interactive systems provide attractive but contradictory features; discretion must be exercised. Under no circumstances, however, should the statement length exceed 65 characters. The rationale here is to maintain independence from a particular compiler, editor, or librarian.

### Identification Division Rules

1. The AUTHOR paragraph must be given in every program. In the program development phase this must include the names of all persons who have written or changed code for the program. The rationale here is to allow quicker access to the originators of a program should problems arise during program development.

2. After a project is beyond the program development phase, as changes are being made comment lines following those for program identification must be updated by appending a brief comment that refers to the software change authorization (SCA) corresponding to the change being made (refer to Chapter 9, Section 9.3). This comment should contain the following:

- SCA numbers corresponding to the changes
- Date that changes actually were made
- Name of person making changes
- Any comments relating to the differences incorporated in that particular version of the module

If other equivalent documentation facilities exist (for example, through the use of an automated librarian), pertinent comment lines may be inserted. The rationale here is to make error detection in operational programs easier. As is often the case, a change made to a program can introduce errors in other program sections. The modification record is a valuable aid in detecting such errors. In addition, as changes are being made, various versions of a given module can be generated. The programming standard will provide for the identification of those versions.

### Data Division Rules

1. All database descriptions contained in the database specification must be maintained in a copy library, external to the processing programs. These descriptions can then be copied into place using the COPY

statement. The rationale here is to place all shared database descriptions in a common library so that all programs that access the data will use correct descriptions with uniform naming conventions.

### Procedure Division Rules

1. All input/output is to be done in separate paragraphs, allowing only one READ statement for each file and only one WRITE statement for each different length and kind of output record. This procedure is enforced by putting all input/output statements within a separate input/output section. For example, use

```
          PERFORM UPDATE-SCAN-TABLES.
          IF (NOT ABORT) OR (NOT END-OF-INPUT)
               PERFORM READ-INPUT.
          IF END-OF-INPUT
               PERFORM SCAN-WRAPUP.

    I-O-SECTION.
    READ-INPUT.
          READ INPUT-FILE
               AT END MOVE 'E' TO INPUT-FILE-
                 STATUS.
          IF   NOT END-OF-INPUT
               ADD 1 TO LINE-COUNT.
```

The rationale here is to isolate those portions of a program that interface with external files.

2. If there is any possibility that the type or value of data that is input external to the system is not correct, and thus can cause an error in subsequent processing, the input must be followed immediately by a test that edits and validates the type or value of the input data. The rationale here is to detect input data errors as soon as they enter the system.

3. The maximum length of any paragraph is 55 lines. The rationale here is to have the length of each paragraph limited to a page of printed text.

4. GO TO statements are not allowed. With some practice, programming without GO TOs becomes quite easy. When you think you need to GO TO, consider: (a) restricting the algorithm, (b) performing blocks of code, (c) copying in a piece of code, (d) repeating a condition previously tested, or (e) reversing a condition to its negative. The rationale here is to force the programmer to *think ahead* and use only 1-in, 1-out control structures. In COBOL this means using the PERFORM, IF, and PERFORM-VARYING-UNTIL constructs for flow of control.

5. The THRU option for PERFORM statements is not allowed. The rationale here is to make the program logic independent of the physical placement of paragraphs.

6. Nesting of IF statements may be three levels deep at most. If deeper nesting is desired, separate procedures should be used.

7. The IF verb can be used for a "multiple-choice" or "case" statement of the form:

```
IF CONDITION-1
     STATEMENT-1
ELSE IF CONDITION-2
     STATEMENT-2
     .
     .
     .
ELSE IF CONDITION-N
     STATEMENT-N.
```

The statements within the case construct must be simple and may not include additional IF statements. The rationale here and in 6 is to avoid having confusing conditional constructs.

8. STOP RUN or EXIT PROGRAM may occur only as the last statement of the main program (that is, the main paragraph or section of the program). The rationale here is to make the logical exit of a program identical to the lexical end of the main program.

9. Parentheses must be used to specify the order of evaluation for the individual conditions of a complex conditional expression. For example, use

```
IF (NOT QUIT-STATE) OR DISPLAY-STATE
   PERFORM RESET-INPUT-BUFFER.
IF ((DISPLAY-LINE-NUM LESS THAN MAX-
     DISPLAY-LENGTH) AND
   (MSG-LENGTH LESS THAN FIELD-SIZE))
   OR UP-CURSOR
     PERFORM PROCESS-MSG.
```

not

```
IF NOT QUIT-STATE OR DISPLAY-STATE
PERFORM RESET-INPUT-BUFFER.
IF DISPLAY-LINE-NUM LESS THAN MAX-DISPLAY-
     LENGTH AND
   MSG-LENGTH LESS THAN FIELD-SIZE OR
     UP-CURSOR
     PERFORM PROCESS-MSG.
```

The rationale here is to make logical operations visible without relying on the often confusing precedence rules.

10. Wherever possible, conditionals should be defined using 88-level definitions in the data division, rather than logical expressions within the conditional procedure statement. The rationale here is to structure the condition details separately from the higher level conditional procedure.

## Cobol Alignment Standards

For displaying the logical structure of a program, the organization of well-spaced programs is critical. Because the time required to space programs may sometimes be laborious, the ultimate solution is an automatic preprocessor for respacing programs according to alignment standards. A sample of such standards is given here.

*General Rules*

1. Between each division, section, or paragraph place a sequence of blank lines that is longer than the maximum sequence of blank lines within the previous division, section, or paragraph.
2. Use at least one blank line between a division header and the first nonblank line of the division.
3. Place division and section headers on a line by themselves starting at column 8.
4. Place paragraph headers on a line by themselves starting at column 8.
5. Do not break words or numeric literals across lines.
6. Indent continuation ines four spaces from the starting column of the initial line.

*Environment Division*

1. Start the computer names of the CONFIGURATION section, the SELECT-NAMES, and I-O CONTROL paragraphs on separate lines starting at column 12.
2. Place subordinate clauses of the SELECT statement and other similar paragraphs on separate lines indented four spaces.

*Data Division*

1. Separate the independent data division aggregates—that is, FD entries along with their following data description entries—by a sequence of blank lines longer than the maximum sequence of blank lines within the previous aggregate.
2. Place at least one blank line before each 01 level data description entry.

3. Start level indicators (FD and 01 level numbers) at column 8.

4. Indent the level numbers of immediately subordinate items of a group item at least two columns (four when possible) from the starting column of the level number of the group item.

5. In an FD entry with multiple clauses, place each clause on a separate line, indenting each clause four spaces from the starting column of the entry name.

6. Do not split nonnumeric literals of a VALUE clause onto a continuation line.

7. If the descriptive clauses of a data description entry do not fit on one line, attempt to indent the starting columns of continuation lines at least two spaces from the starting column of the last descriptive clause.

*Procedure Division*

1. Do not place two or more statements on one line. The ony exception is for lengthy sequences of short statements logically grouped in pairs or triples on one line.

2. Align the starting columns of the statements making up a sentence and the sentences making up a paragraph. The general rule is to align logically parallel constructs.

3. Align the word ELSE in a conditional statement with the corresponding word IF. Indent the statements in the IF part and the ELSE part at least four spaces.

4. Place phrases such as AT END, WHEN, INVALID KEY, GIVING, USING, TALLYING, VARYING, UNTIL, and AFTER on separate lines, indenting the start of each phrase at least four spaces.

5. List each procedure (level 2) performed by the main program (level 1) immediately after the main procedure. Subsequent procedures (level 3) performed by a procedure in level 2 must be listed just after level 2, and so forth. Within levels, the order of listing is up to the user. Two exceptions are allowed: (1) procedures called from several levels and (2) procedures that logically are related (for example, I/O routines). These may be grouped as desired by the programmer.

## The COPY Feature

One of the most effective features of COBOL is the COPY verb. In brief, the COPY verb allows the insertion of program text from an external library. This feature has many advantages for writing large systems.

The format of the COPY statement is simple:

$$\texttt{COPY TEXT-NAME} \left\{ \begin{array}{l} \texttt{ON} \\ \texttt{IN} \end{array} \right\} \texttt{LIBRARY NAME}$$

The effect of compilation of a COPY statement is to replace the COPY statement by text written in the COBOL library. The COBOL library may contain three types of entries:

1. Entries for the identification or environment division giving security comments or equipment-oriented information.
2. Entries for the data division giving descriptions of files, reports, or working-storage items.
3. Entries for the procedure division giving procedures or sections for commonly used routines

The advantages of using the COPY verb backed up by a suitable library are many:

1. Descriptions of external files may be copied into place, thus ensuring that all programs that use the files have *identical* descriptions. This also ensures uniform program names for objects in the files.
2. The use of standard user-defined words for a given project can be enforced by copying their description into working storage.
3. The use of standard procedures for input/output, file updating, and so forth, can be facilitated.
4. Writing of programs can be simplified, as the user need not type in segments of code given in the library.
5. Errors can be reduced, because once the library entries are correct all accessing programs will be correct.
6. The entire programming effort can proceed more quickly as the library facility grows to handle more cases.

Thus with a sufficiently developed library, the COPY feature can significantly upgrade the entire programming process, allowing the rapid development and cost-effective support of high-quality programs.

## Summary

The foregoing standards are a sample effort to promote high-quality COBOL programs. This concern is a familiar one to all managers and programmers who face day-to-day problems in the development of software systems. Although the adoption of good programming conventions is only a part of the effort to produce high-quality software, we believe that the standards given here are a solid step in the right direction.

## 7.4 FORTRAN STANDARDS

FORTRAN is the grandfather of algebraically oriented languages; its use was already established as early as 1958. Over the years it has evolved into a standard language for scientific programming projects. An official standard issued by ANSI in 1966 has enjoyed wide acceptance by the computer industry. This standardization made it possible to transport FORTRAN programs developed on one computer to another computer without significant modifications. Gradually, FORTRAN applications broadened from strictly numerically oriented problems to more general applications involving character and file manipulations. This evolution made it necessary to extend the capabilities of the FORTRAN language. In 1977 ANSI issued an enhanced FORTRAN standard that includes the 1966 standard as a subset. Today both FORTRAN 66 and FORTRAN 77 are used, depending on the particular compiler version supported by various operating systems.

### Transportability Criteria

Transportability is one of the most attractive aspects of any standard language. The maturity and wide acceptance of FORTRAN makes it particularly attractive as a portable language. In certain cases, however, total transportability is not actually realized. There are usually some machine-dependent aspects to be considered when a language is moved from one machine to another. The ability to divide machine-dependent and -independent attributes into separate entities by subprograms greatly enhances the transferability of programs. Furthermore, the ability to compile these entities individually aids in the speedy checkout of transferred modules. Programs may be written as a collection of smaller routines, compiled and tested individually, and put together in building-block fashion into large assemblages without recompilation. In this way, machine-dependent code may be economically isolated into separate modules. Typical machine-dependent functions may be:

- Precision of variables
- Special input/output
- Error checking and recovery
- Operating system interfaces
- Particularly stringent real-time applications

### Coding Techniques and Rules

Paradoxically, the more clever the programmer, the less likely that transportable code will be produced. That is, many commonly used techniques or "tricks" in FORTRAN programming are severely detrimental to program transportability because of implementation differences inherent to individual compilers. The following is a list of some practices of techniques that generally should be avoided to assure the generation of transportable code.

1. A DO loop should not be terminated with a complex statement as an IF. Many compilers that allow termination of DO loops of IF statements disclaim the predictability of results.
2. One terminal statement for several nested DO loops should be avoided. Some compilers put special restrictions on nested DO loops that terminate on one statement. For example, a particular compiler may only allow the innermost DO to transfer directly to its termination point.
3. Compilers may have inherent table size restrictions on character length. Therefore, literal strings of length greater than 255 characters should be avoided.
4. Altering a DO parameter within a loop may produce varying results depending on particular compiler mechanization of the DO. Therefore, it is generally a good practice not to alter a DO parameter within a loop.
5. Testing for floating-point zero is a risky practice and should not be done. Example:

   ```
   IF(X.EQ.0.0)GO TO 10.
   ```

   Because of inherent inaccuracies of floating-point representations, a test for a specific number may fail when it actually should pass.
6. Ambiguous statements such as

   ```
   N = N+FUNC(N)*N
   ```

   where FUNC(N) alters N depending on the particular implementation of the compiler's scanning algorithm. If the original value of N is not stored in another temporary location, FUNC(N) may destroy it.
7. Compiler implementation of division by zero may vary. Division by zero may result in values zero, $10^{39}$, and so forth, or may generate an error condition depending on the system. It should not be assumed that some finite value will result from division by zero.
8. Most compilers do not allow recursive subroutines. They usually are difficult to support and should not be used.
9. Some compilers will not handle missing arguments (variable length) in a subroutine CALL successfully. Generally the number of arguments is assumed to be fixed. Therefore, it is generally

wise to avoid variable-length argument strings in subroutine CALLS.

10. Incremental compilers cannot handle scattered type, dimension, and DATA statements.
11. Do not assume a loop is always executed once. Example:

```
DO 10 I = 4, N
```

where N=3. Loops of the form DO 10 I = K, J, where J K may or may not be executed once depending on where the test for completion is implemented.

12. Using large numbers as DO indices may cause problems in compilers in which the DO loops are implemented in index registers, thereby setting an upper limit on index values. Example:

```
DO 10 I = 1, N
```

where $N = 2^{17}$.

13. Never transfer into a DO range. Most compilers do not guarantee the results of transfers into a DO loop.
14. Do not assume that an incorrect computed GO TO variable will result in a default condition such as "falling through." Some compilers generate code for testing the computed GO TO arguments. The last statement label or next statement becomes the error condition default.

Some additional rule-of-thumb guidelines are:

1. Avoid usage of extensions to the standard being used. This includes avoiding FORTRAN 77 capabilities that are not part of FORTRAN 66, if that is the standard to be used.
2. Document extensively all dialect variations and machine-dependent code, functions.
3. Modularize programs into machine-dependent and -independent sections.
4. The FORTRAN external procedure permits interfacing to a non-FORTRAN subprogram. This provides the capability of allowing subprograms written in assembler language (or another higher level language) to be referenced by a FORTRAN 77 program unit. Such interfacing should be done by strict adherence to FORTRAN 77 procedural rules. In the use of FORTRAN 66, it is good practice to avoid assembly language code interfaces.
5. Do not use programming tricks that depend on machine idiosyncrasies.
6. Design magnetic tape outputs for general compatibility. Avoid complicated blocking or binary outputs.

7. Always initialize storage; never depend on the system to do this for you.
8. Always assume the character set is variable. Do not make programs dependent on the internal character representation of a particular machine.
9. Plan to end the implementation phase with a test package (that is, a regression test set) that can be used in future transfers.
10. Estimate the range of data values and document them. The precision of integer and floating-point arithmetic in FORTRAN is machine and software dependent. If other systems to which the program is to be transferred have fewer bits assigned to the mantissa in floating-point representations, for example, the current data may generate over- or underflows. These could go undetected, causing an inherent "gremlin" in the transferred program.

## 7.5 SUMMARY

The preceding sections should provide some insights into the development of programming standards. Although the examples offered cover COBOL and FORTRAN, the concepts are transferable to other languages, assuming the features exist to support the standards. We believe that language design should be based on a substantial knowledge of production programming standards. And that is the purpose of standardization committees, to revise and refine the language to support desired production standards as they evolve.

# CHAPTER 8

# Software Testing and Quality Control

## 8.1 INTRODUCTION

This chapter's principal theme is that effective computer software testing and quality control procedures require the same level of management control as does writing the software. Software must be tested to identify faults and to confirm the correctness of its performance—*before the system is made operational!* Quality control (with emphasis on *control*) is the process by which operational software is built and maintained at an acceptable level of quality. Every aspect of a system's development and operational use must be handled with appropriate care, with no exceptions for these two supporting functions.

This chapter also advances a secondary theme, that test requirements can be identified as natural extensions of the system's design requirements. In addition, a system's test library is a principal tool of the quality control procedural package.

The chapter addresses the subjects of software testing and quality control within the framework of the incremental method. Thus considerable detail has been applied to management control over incremental development and use of software testing to establish and maintain quality control.

## 8.2 BACKGROUND RATIONALE

There are far too many examples of data systems that do not provide the service required by the system's users. Each of these faulty systems fails, to some degree, to perform in terms of the following qualitative definitions:

- *Availability*: to provide the functions and services requested by the users
- *Reliability*: to provide accurate and dependable functional outputs required by the users
- *Maintainability*: to provide services supported by rapid recovery after failure

A system's inability to meet any of these performance measures usually can be traced to one of the following: faulty design, improper development, or inadequate maintenance provisions. These deficiencies often are not discovered until the system is operational, owing mainly to lack of appropriate testing and inadequate quality control planning during the system's development.

Software is particularly vulnerable to poor performance when it is inadequately tested. It's effectiveness has proved difficult to verify within the system development process. Successful software testing is tied directly to design of the system. Quality of the design is likely to have greater impact on project success than quality of work at any other stage. The following design elements are essential:

- Documentation of each module must be prepared in depth and must be complete before programming is begun.
- Software testing plans and procedures must be developed in the same phase as the system design.
- Test data required to test the software must be meticulously selected as representative of the full range of live data.
- Preliminary correctness of each module is the responsibility of the programmer. Final certification, however, must be performed by someone other than the original programmer.

The means for proving software effectiveness must be prepared in conjunction with the software design. Also, the facilities to support software maintenance and future changes must be built into the system; therefore, planning for quality control must start no later than the design phase. If a top-down approach is employed in the software design and development, the preparation of tests and quality control procedures must track this top-down process.

## 8.3 A MEASURE OF SOFTWARE QUALITY

As an aid to defining the lifecycle control problem, we subscribe to the measure of software quality described by Cave and Salisbury (1978). Although this is a more quantitative approach than that of Wilbur (1981), many of the conclusions are the same. Software quality, as defined here, can only be measured after IOC in a live operational environment. Before IOC, software quality can be predicted and controlled by measuring factors that affect it; however, the measure of quality offered here is considered essential in correlating the effects of such factors.

We start with the notion that quality is proportional to system availability, $A$, and inversely proportional to the cost of maintaining that availability, $M$:

$$Q = \frac{A}{1 + M}. \quad (1)^*$$

The cost to maintain a system is directly measurable in the environments considered. To define availability as used in Equation 1, we first define factors $f_i$ that describe the relative importance of all system functions as judged by the user. These factors can be normalized such that

$$\sum_{i=1}^{n} f_i = 1, \quad (2)$$

where $n$ is the number of functions that must be available to the user. We define $l_i$ as the level of availability of function $i$ such that

$$0 \leqq l_i \leqq 1. \quad (3)$$

If $l_i$ is one (zero), then the system is totally available (unavailable), and levels can take on binary or continuous values. If all system functions are totally available, then

$$\sum f_i \cdot l_i = \sum f_i = 1. \quad (4)$$

It is the user who must define the relative importance of functions of the system as well as their level of availability at any time.

We now define instantaneous system availability as

$$A(t) = \sum f_i \cdot l_i(t), \quad (5)$$

noting that software quality changes with time. Although quality as we have defined it may fluctuate, in the long run it generally improves. To measure availability practically, we must select a reasonable time increment. Referring to Figure 8.1, consider that we will take measure-

*The unit is added only because the cost of maintenance theoretically could vanish.

ments over successive time intervals of length $t_f - t_0$. A practical increment may be one month. During these intervals, we will continuously measure the availability level of each system function. We assume that all functions are totally available unless it is determined that their availability levels fall below unity. For example, in Figure 8.1 at time $t_{kd}$, the availability of function *i* drops to some value less than 1. At time $t_{ku}$, the problem is corrected, and the function is totally available to the user. For ease of defining average availability over the interval $(t_0, t_f)$, we define unavailability as

$$u_i = 1 - l_i. \tag{6}$$

We can now obtain average availability for the total system over the period $(t_0, t_f)$ as

$$A = 1 - \frac{1}{t_f - t_0} \sum_i \sum_k f_i u_{ki} \tau_{ki}, \tag{7}$$

where $u_{ki}$ is the *k*th malfunction of function $f_i$, and $\tau_{ki}$ is the duration of the *k*th malfunction from time of discovery to time of correction. We thus have a measure of average system availability over a given time interval. Knowing the cost of maintenance over the same time interval, we then can compute a value for quality.

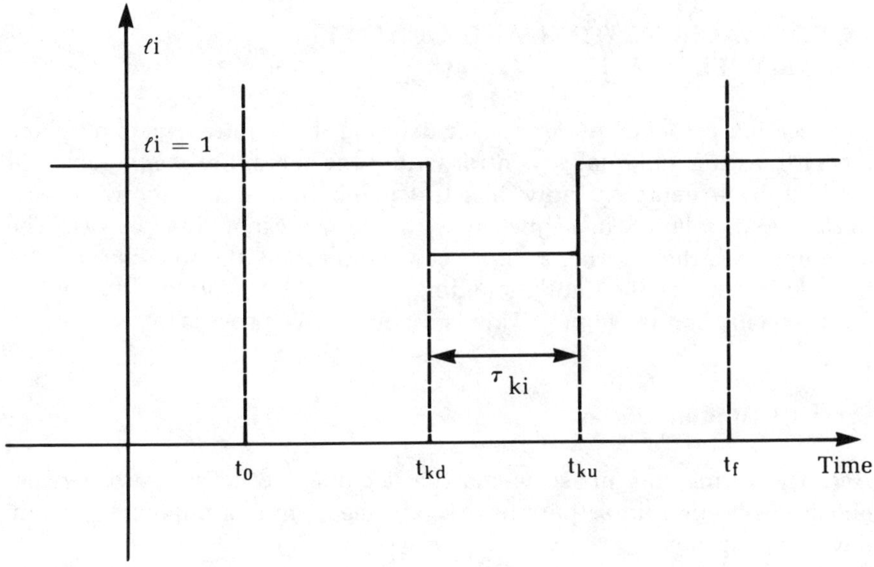


**Figure 8.1.** Level of Availability of Function $f_i$.

As an alternative, it may be meaningful to define $M'$ as a relative cost of restorative maintenance where

$$M' = \frac{\text{support budget consumed by restorative maintenance}}{\text{total support budget}} \tag{8}$$

leading to

$$Q' = \frac{A}{1 + M'} \tag{9}$$

as a more universal measure of quality, ranging between 0 and 1.† This approach is based on the experience that the budgeted cost of restorative maintenance is normally small compared with the total support budget allotted for functional changes and enhancements.

The measures of quality offered are not intended to be absolute. Their shortcomings, such as interdependencies among functions, can be overcome by good judgment in determining the levels of availability. If one keeps a log of individual values of functional availability, then one can compute a new set of quality factors on changing the relative weights of functional importance; however, the significance of the measures lies with their interpretation. Note that availability can be improved by shortening the time it takes to bring a reduced level of availability back to unity; however, such efforts can increase the cost of maintenance and thereby offset potential improvements in the overall measure of quality.

## 8.4 SOFTWARE TESTING AND QUALITY CONTROL PLANNING

This section presents guidelines for defining the requirements and plans for both testing and quality control within the context of the incremental method. Statements on individual test plans and quality control procedures are presented in sequence with the corresponding phases. The assumption is that, during each succeeding phase within the incremental method, a more refined understanding of the testing and quality control requirements can be gained. This is a cumulative process.

### Project Definition Phase

Activity during this phase yields the documented definition of system objectives, constraints, parameters, strategy, and preliminary system development plan.

---

†Suggested by R. McHenry, IBM Corporation, in private communication.

*Testing and Quality Control Considerations*

1. *Initial identification:* It is appropriate at this time simply to review the problem definition and identify areas within the preliminary system description that will require some form of testing. For example, if the system is to have real-time capability, a corresponding plan can be set for real-time testing.

2. *Related systems:* It may be appropriate during this phase to review other operational systems considered to have similar objectives and applications. Identify and note the methods used to test and maintain these systems.

3. *Development plan:* The preliminary system development plan requires only identification and gross scheduling of subsystem tests, full-system tests, and parallel tests.

## Functional Specification Phase

Activity during this phase yields a set of system functional requirements and an updated system development plan.

*Testing and Quality Control Considerations*

1. *Test criteria:* Before the functional specifications are documented, it is necessary to interview user personnel about their current and desired information-handling capability. Most responses to interview questions affect the testing and quality control requirements as well as system design requirements. Consider that each functional requirement can also be translated into a "test-to" criterion. For example, if the user's present system is automated, ask about the response-to-inquiry time. The new system, when tested, ordinarily will have to equal and probably beat the old response time.

2. *User environment:* Determine how the user's present system is maintained and enhanced. This information will help identify constraints that may be imposed on the maintenance and change control procedures by the user's organization and operating environment.

3. *Requirements:* Because no individual or group can possibly remember the various potential test parameters and constraints required of a large system, it is best to record this information as it is uncovered. Test parameters and performance constraints form a major part of the functional specifications. Quantitative criteria may be necessary to further delineate the system's functional specifications. Examples of quantitative criteria are desired mean time between failure and desired mean time to repair.

4. *Plan update:* The updated system development plan should include any specific notations that can be made at this time about testing and quality control procedures. Activity titles in the plan should correspond to the terms used as testing and quality control procedures.

## Environment Specification Phase

Activity during this phase yields hardware/software environment specifications, an initial system documentation set, and an updated project plan.

*Testing and Quality Control Considerations*

1. *Test environment specification:* The testing environment must be described in precise terms. Considerable evaluation must precede the selection of hardware, system software, and the development support software environment. Virtually the same level of effort must be made to evaluate and trade off the test environment. Additional parameters and environmental constraints, such as the computer capacity and application language, must be included in the evaluation. Refer to the following section, "System Design Phase," for additional considerations.

2. *Walk-throughs:* The information gathered in the preliminary documentation set provides the first opportunity for a paper evaluation or "walk-through" of the system specifications against the test parameters and the operating environment constraints. The objective of this walk-through is to determine the adequacy and relevance of the test parameters and constraints. Separate individuals should determine whether there is one or more tests for each functional specification and whether each test is expressed in relevant, quantitative terms.

3. *Quality control comparisons:* A similar comparison can be made between the initial documentation set and the proposed quality control procedures.

4. *Review of technical approach:* Another reason for performing these walk-throughs is to raise the user's level of confidence in the technical approach selected. The system's analysts should be able to state convincingly that they are sure of how to satisfy the user's needs. The results of these walk-throughs should also reinforce the justification for entering the system design phase.

From project definition through environment specification, the activity related to system testing and quality control have involved requirements definition, comparison, and evaluation. This cumulative process is required to minimize technical oversight. The results of these activities will be used in the next phase, system design.

## System Design Phase

This activity yields a complete external system documentation set, a detailed test plan, an initial quality control plan, and a detailed program development plan with "build" schedules.

*Testing and Quality Control Considerations*

1. Three important considerations should be mentioned first:

- The system test library must be documented as precisely as the final software documentation.
- Change control procedures must be developed and imposed at the outset of the design phase as the first and principal element of quality control. Changes in functional or environment specifications must be initiated only for justifible cause and executed under tight management control.
- The following outline is general and must be tailored to the specific application.

2. *Development test plan:* The development test plan and supporting activity schedule should complement and be as formal as the software development plan and schedule. As a mimimum, the test plan should identify:

- The system by title and nomenclature, with appropriate cross-references to the external documentation set and development plan.
- The organization/personnel responsible for preparing the plan, the organization responsible for implementing and executing test, and the organizations that are to evaluate and approve the test results.
- A general overview or test philosophy that includes: testing objectives in terms of software performance, constraints imposed by the system's configuration, equipment and software availability, contractual considerations, and the methods selected for performing and verifying the tests.
- The identification and sequence of the various tests, identification of the product, and the report or activity milestone that signifies the end of each test.
- Listings of computer test tools, equipments, testing procedures, and physical locations for conducting the tests.
- A detailed statement on specification change control procedures.

The test plan is to be used as one of the principal references for developing the test library and quality control procedures.

3. *Test schedule:* The testing schedule should be prepared in conjunction with final review of the system documentation. By producing the test schedule before the program development or "build" schedule, the sequence of programming activities is brought into perspective directly. The rationale is that specific modules, programs, and supporting subsystems must be available to perform a test. It follows that these items must be identified along with their availability schedules in order to meet the test. Again, dates and durations of individual developments and tests must be included in the program development and test schedule when changes are considered. The development and test schedules are also management control documents.

4. *Testing process:* The testing process from the user's viewpoint is the reverse of the top-down development process (see, for example, Sherr, 1972). The general sequence is as follows:

User requirements definition
System design
Subsystem design
Module design and code
Module test
Subsystem test
System test
User operations

The objective of this process is to identify errors early in the sequence, where they can be corrected with the least expense. The basic philosophy is build, prove through testing, fix if faulty, add to, and test with the previously proven modules and programs. This is also a top-down process as explained in Section 3.1.

5. *Walk-through:* The best guard against incorporating an undetected error into the design is the walk-through. It is invariably less costly to spend the time and effort to confirm the soundness of a system's design than to rework the system after it has been built. The walk-through, performed on a group or unbiased individual basis, is an excellent test of the design before the design phase is terminated.

6. *Test library:* A major feature of the incremental development concept is the test library described in the next section. Briefly, the test library is the computer-assisted test tools plus the complete documentation of test parameters, tests, their limitations, and reported results for every module and subsystem. The test plan is the cornerstone of the test library development. The test schedule is obviously both the chronicle of past events and a forecast of the future. Growth of the test library must reflect the testing plan and process in the following manner:

| *Phase* | *Test* | *Activity* |
|---|---|---|
| Development | Module | Individual program modules machine tested and debugged |
| | System integration | Total system integrated to check out under volume transactions and to determine capacity and dynamics |
| Operational testing | Parallel | Total system installed under an environment parallel to that planned under live operation, with the use, if possible, of live input to track a true parallel operation |
| | Acceptance | Full-cycle tests conducted to demonstrate performance in terms of operating capability, availability, and dependability |
| Support | Regression | Full-cycle regression test library maintained and ready to go for each new change |

7. *Quality control plan:* Quality control is the planned and concerted effort to maintain system integrity and identity, along with service, at an acceptable performance level and an affordable cost. Like the development and test plans, a quality control plan must be tailored to the system it supports. During the design phase, an initial control plan must be prepared.

Four activities within a system's lifecycle must be controlled to assure the system's performance:

- *Development:* design and construction of the software
- *Operational maintenance:* fixing programs that fail during normal operation so that they will provide the service intended
- *Software refinement:* modifying programs to improve the performance of one or more existing functions
- *Software enhancement:* modifying existing programs or creating new programs to support one or more new functions

8. *Plan contents:* The quality control plan should have the same attributes of formality and compatibility as the other plans and schedules. It is to be used as the principal reference for writing quality control procedures. As a minimum it should identify:

- The system by title and nomenclature
- The organization/personnel responsible for directing the quality control program and for the training user and support personnel, together with the qualifications for training and the job descriptions for the support functions
- A general overview to include: quality control objectives as they relate to the particular system, with a careful definition of development, maintenance, refinement, and enhancement in terms of the system's needs
- Use of the system documentation libraries and test libraries to perform error detection and analysis, with emphasis on the pertinent areas (e.g., recovery procedures, etc.)
- The functional specification and documentation change control procedure
- The test library maintenance procedure
- The operational/performance audit procedure and attendant reports
- Quality control training and implementation schedules

## Program Development Phase

During this phase individual program modules are coded, tested, integrated as functional programs, and retested. Coding is accomplished in response to the objectives and sequence prescribed in the development plan. The test library is constructed. Testing is accomplished in accordance with the test plan and schedule. The hardware, communications, and peripheral equipment are acquired, installed, and checked out. The system test plan is updated for the operational test phase.

*Testing and Quality Control Considerations*

1. *Change control implementation:* The efforts put into test library planning, development, scheduling, and quality control procedures are challenged during this phase. First, change control must operate properly at the outset, or program rewriting efforts will result in chaos. It is assumed that better planning will result in fewer changes. It must also be assumed that some factor has been overlooked and that changes will occur.

2. *System test library:*The stystem test library must be developed and documented during this phase in conjunction with program coding. This is the ideal time for this activity because the responsible programmers now will have the opportunity to tune test procedures to the software as well as the system documentation. The object is to develop sequential procedures that will exercise and demonstrate the system's capability to respond to both partial and complete functional requirements. The procedures, when used, should show predictable results using both good and bad data as well as good and bad operating methods. Refer to the detailed description of the system test library and techniques in the prior section.)

3. *Operational test plan:* During the latter part of the development phase, the test plan and procedures should be evaluated to determine their effectiveness for the operational test plan. Any revisions that are required should be made. This review is to aid in preparation of the operational test plan, which is the cornerstone of the operational testing phase. It fully specifies the acceptance test sequence, required personnel training, equipment deployment, and system activation. If the previous plans and results have been documented adequately, the final writing should involve no more than a recompilation of the pertinent "test-to" requirements, development scenarios, test reporting formats, and acceptance requirements. Particular attention should be given to testing the modules and subsystems that have been subjected to change during development. It must be verified that the full-cycle regression test library has been maintained and that changes have been properly integrated.

## Operational Testing Phase

During this phase, selected user operating and support personnel are trained for participation in the tests. Full systems tests are conducted, and quality control procedures, system documentation library, and test library are finalized.

*Testing and Quality Control Considerations*

1. *User's exposure to system:* If this phase could be conducted within totally ideal circumstances, system capability would be demonstrated to

show anticipated results and they simply would be accepted. In practice, it is common for the user to finally see (at this late date) exactly what services the system is designed to provide. The user then realizes what he must pay in terms of revised organization, policies, and procedures. Although he previously may have been told what to expect, now he can see the process for himself. The sequence of tests should be conducted in such a way that the user is given ample opportunity to observe, gain understanding, and comment on the demonstrated service. A vital consideration for successful testing and implementation is early exposure of the user, who must be assisted to appreciate the system's limitations as well as its advantages.

2. *Test bed:* If operational tests are performed in a test-bed environment, the final acceptance tests should be performed on the target operating facilities. There may have been some technical accommodation (such as a translator) made to simulate "live" operations on the test bed that are not required in the operating environment. There may be a difference in software performance on the two facilities. These differences must be resolved in favor of the "live" operating system.

3. *Quality control plan:* The initial quality control plan, prepared during the design phase, is formalized now. The procedures incorporated in the plan must be executed and evaluated during operational tests. Those procedures that pass the evaluation are formally documented and included in the training programs for operating and support personnel.

4. *Quality control during tests:* Often there is a temptation during this phase to make changes in an expedient manner to gain the system's acceptance. Not every system requirement, however, will be met during the acceptance test. It can also be anticipated that additional functional capabilities may be requested just before or during the tests. Any major deficiency must be resolved before final acceptance. Action on minor deficiencies and additional capabilities should be deferred until after testing because knowledge of the whole picture may modify the changes. In both situations quality control procedures must be enforced to assure the system's overall performance and integrity. Only after formal test and acceptance can the system be considered ready for live operation.

### Installation and Support Phase

During this phase the system is installed and activiated according to the implementation plan and schedule. Production (operations) control procedures are implemented under an appropriate operations coordinator or system manager. A system continuation plan is prepared and maintained as the reference document for controlling system operation, performance evaluation, system change, and ultimately the transition form the current system to its replacement.

*Quality Control Considerations*

1. *Implementation:* Between the time a system is accepted for installation and the time it is phased out, production and quality control are the two major functions of the system's manager. Under an operating philosophy, the maintenance, software refinements, and software enhancements are subordinated to the quality control plan. Software modification efforts, including the full range of testing and formal release for use, are to be considered a logical extension of the change control procedure. The system's test library is one of the tools that support these modifications. As changes are incorporated, the test and documentation libraries must be maintained accordingly. The significant concept of quality control is that both availability and quality of the system's service must be deliberately managed.

2. *System performance log:* Adequate documentation of system performance should be maintained during the system's operating life. A performance log, the system's performance specifications, performance audit report, operations status reports, and those change requests that were not acted on will provide an excellent source of information for defining the current status.

## 8.5 TESTING TECHNIQUES

The preceding section provided general guidelines for developing and implementing the system test library and quality control as defined within the incremental method. This section identifies several methods and techniques that generally are applicable to development, testing, and control of software support.

It should be understood that there are almost as many testing methods as there are programming languages. No method is best, but those discussed here have evolved successfully. These apply to real-time, interactive, data-based information systems. This section addresses the subject of testing in terms of software testing philosophy, techniques, user participation, and acceptance. The ultimate objective is to ensure user acceptance of the system.

### General Considerations

1. *Testing philosophy:* A testing philosophy lays down the rationale for identifying test requirements and for developing and executing tests. The obvious but often neglected rationale for testing is:

- User requirements will change.
- The system will have errors.

- Revisions and modifications will occur before all of the system requirements are met.
- Changes will introduce new problems and errors.
- Errors can be costly during live operation.

System test requirements, which must be specific, grow from three simple propositions:

- Functional specification: What must the system do?
- Performance requirements: How frequent and fast must the system perform these functions? What are the tolerances, if any?
- Environment specifications: What constraints are imposed on the system's development/operating environment? When can testing be done? What equipments and support software can be used?

The system test should demonstrate:

- Functional performance with acceptable error
- Performance in time with acceptable degradation
- Suitability of the testing environment

Ground rules for conducting a test are:

- To qualify as valid, a test must be repeatable under prescribed conditions and testing environments.
- A test is not complete until all requirements are satisfied—that is, a go-no go condition, pass or fail.
- Tests are to be conducted as formally as possible, with the testing activity visible to everyone concerned.
- All test slippages must be reported, together with an analysis of the cause and, if necessary, the planned remedial action.

2. *Staffing:* Personnel assignments for system testing should be divided on the basis of three areas of responsibility:

- Preparation of test requirements in accordance with the functional and performance requirements; preparation of the test plan and requirements for test data
- Preparation of the detailed test data, scenarios, and documentation in response to the requirements and in conjunction with the design; maintainance of the test set
- Testing of the program modules after they are coded; reporting the results. Testing and excerising of the integrated subsystems to measure performance against the capabilities of the integrated system (which should be done independently from 2 above)

## Special Considerations

Major errors stem from improper interpretation either of functional requirements or their translation during the design phase. Such mistakes do not stem from coding logic errors. As a result, software for an interactive, database system requires comprehensive testing conducted under well-conceived and -controlled procedures to minimize the risks of major errors and poor integration of programs.

These systems are complex because of a high degree of user interface, sophisticated systems software, communications, and concurrent processing of multiple transactions based on random demand. Variations on the following procedure can be devised to deal effectively with these complexities:

1. *Module or program testing:* The purpose of these tests is to search for and correct module logic/coding errors.
2. *Integration testing:* These tests are applied to integrated modules, or to programs to check out subsystem logic and operation of one or more complete system functions, including indicated errors.
3. *Single-thread testing:* A single input data stream is added to the system, and single transactions are sequentially entered and processed to further check out and verify the system's logic and individual functions.
4. *Multithread testing:* These tests require multiterminal simulation for entering multiple inputs concurrently to detect errors arising from simultaneous processing of a variety of transactions. Database update and inquiry modules will require input in both correct and incorrect order to properly excerise editing and control procedures.
5. *Volume testing:* A simulator can be used to apply a heavy volume of representative transactions on the system. All the file processing and other functions must be exercised to ensure that the cumulative results are correct. These test runs must simulate actual operating cycles, including system failure and recovery.
6. *Field testing:* Remote entry and receiving terminals must be installed to check out data-communications networks in all transmission modes. The terminals must be operated by both project and user personnel under near-actual conditions to check on the system's ability to handle variations and errors caused by the operators.

## Techniques

1. *Top-down testing:* The testing process discussed in Section 8.4 (system design phase) may appear to be bottom-up because input control modules must be developed before any testing can be started. These modules may include state control, input edit, transaction validation and control, and database updates. Such modules may require support programs that simulate the input of data and inquiry transactions (e.g., from a terminal). These modules must be designed and developed to the point that at least sequential functions or transactions can be processed. They should contain program exits or stubs for those modules that will be added in the future. Once these major modules are adequately tested and debugged, subordinate modules are added to the major modules and tested. It is this process that must be performed top-down.

At this point we should put to rest the issue of top-down versus bottom-up testing. Certainly Sherr's (1972) approach to testing satisfies what generally is considered the best way to construct and test a system during the program development phase. Yet, Sherr calls this method "bottom-up" and clearly justifies it. On the other hand, this approach as we have interpreted it satisfies the common definition of top-down testing. The discrepancy is easily explained: It merely depends on the viewpoint taken—that is, the functional (user) viewpoint or the implementation (developer) viewpoint. Design must be top-down from the functional standpoint, starting with the major outputs the user desires. Testing, on the other hand, must be top-down from the implementation standpoint—that is, top control and input modules first, reporting last. As it turns out, this approach appears "bottom-up" from the user viewpoint, which is Scherr's stance for both design and testing. Because the top-down testing sequence is a mirror image, *in reverse order*, of the top-down design process, it is obvious that implementation/testing cannot start until the design is complete.

2. *Regression testing:* Regression testing is a fault isolation technique that has proved successful in assuring software integrity while additional functions are introduced. The technique should be considered as a formal testing procedure. It is consistant with the top-down approach.

The regression principal is to rerun previous successful tests (before adding new functional tests) to measure the effects of a software modification once it has been integrated. In practice, new modules that have been individually tested are compiled with the previously tested major modules. First, the previous functional (regression) tests are run to determine if the presence of the new modules causes any problems. After the anticipated results are obtained, the functional tests for the new modules are applied in conjunction with rerun of the previous tests, or "tested base," to ensure the integrity and capability of the total system.

The regression test sequence is a natural course to use with a top-down approach.

To recap, the scheduled sequence for adding functions should be:

- Build and test next level of modules.
- Integrate these modules.
- Perform regression tests with tested base.
- Test new function with rerun of augmented regression tests.
- Repeat procedural cycle until all functions have been added and accepted.

This "growing" procedure is carried over to the system's operational phase to be used in conjunction with the total system test set to support software quality control.

3. *Benchmark testing:* Performance requirements or comparisons are best measured using a set of benchmark tests. Benchmark tests should be designed to provide a clear measure of system response to input and processing functions that cover the time spectrum. These tests should be extensive enough so that their results define the crossover points of system response versus requirement satisfaction.

4. *Test scenarios:* Test scenarios of single and combined functions have proved useful as structured test procedures. A script is prepared that identifies the user and operating environments. It prescribes the transactions, initiation, input, throughput (including file identification), and output. A good scenario instructs the test conductor to make a variety of errors, as well as to correct inquiries. The survey information gathered on the potential user's personnel, operations, current system, and tests applied to similar systems should provide a good basis for writing realistic scenario scripts. These scenarios, refined after use in the testing environment, are useful as training tools and as part of the quality control package for use in regression tests.

5. *Walk-throughs:* Walk-throughs, as discussed in prior sections, are an economical technique for determining the validity and completeness of the specifications and planned tests. They can be accomplished in a variety of ways. One type of walk-through is simulated by a group of people working their way through the functional specifications, system documentation set, and program code, using a test case or scenario. Creating a matrix by listing the system functions on one axis and the modules in logical order on the other axis also may be desirable. The matrix then can be filled in to show where the modules implement and support each function. In addition, one may require the listing of inputs and outputs and a comparison of the lists to the code to derive cause-effect relationships. To avoid excessive and costly reruns, walk-throughs also should be required practice during the trouble-shooting of operational failures. These walk-throughs can be done if one has access to a computer-generated error

report, a printout of the affected modules showing the status of the transaction when a failure occurred, and the system documentation library.

6. *System test library:* The following test library items and documentation should be available for testing and quality control for each module and subsystem.

- A specification title page, with the date of preparation and signatures of the analyst and programmer
- The latest test output, dated, with the name of the person performing the test and containing listings of the printed transaction outputs with all controls
- The most recent specification change and release notices, with test requirements and test data
- Pertinent preceding test output sets and specification changes in reverse date order
- The most recent complete documentation for the module, with program listing, interface specifications, test requirements, and test data
- The control language listing for the operating system

If testing is conducted in a uniform manner, it is likely that any differences in output or any software failures can be attributed to the last "fix" or specification change.

7. *Testing aids:* There are almost as many testing aids as there are application systems. Available aids developed for previous applications will not work precisely for the next application, no matter how similar, without some adaptation. If existing computer equipment, attendant supporting software, and a proven compiler language are selected for a new system, the development risk is moderate. If, on the other hand, new unproven equipment and software are to be used in an application, or any of the applicable aids must be highly modified or newly developed, the risk goes up.

Among the variety of aids available, some are especially useful if a test bed is to be maintained to support the operational system. A number of facilities are described in Chapter 10. Section 10.4.

# CHAPTER 9

# Software Product Support

## 9.1 INTRODUCTION

Many authorities state that 80% of the efforts devoted to software are expended on existing product support. This is because successful software products are constantly subject to change and evolution. The economic reality of software lifecycles is that requests, which necessitate changes and revisions, will be made by the users throughout the life of the product. As the product matures and user experience broadens, enhancements to the product will be introduced continually.

The software end product, defined in Section 1.7, usually represents the major assets of a software company. These assets must be protected in the same manner as any highly valuable assets to ensure that their value is maintained and, in the case of software, continually enhanced. To accomplish this, all changes must be carefully documented and controlled.

## 9.2 SYSTEM ACTION REQUESTS

After a software product is installed into a customer's site, problems will arise that will necessitate vendor action. This situation will occur regardless of the preinstallation testing rigor. Some reported problems will be deficiencies within the software, for which remedies will be necessary. Other reports will result from misunderstandings, improper user operations, and so forth. As the product matures, most requests will be for improvements in system functional or performance capabilities. The basic objective in dealing with such requests for support is to satisfy the customer in a timely and efficient manner.

Initial requests for action directed to the software support organization are defined herein as system action requests (SAR). These requests can be divided broadly into three categories: correction of deficiencies, refinements, and enhancements or change of function scope. The categories are defined in the following paragraphs.

### Correction of Deficiencies

Requests for correction of deficiences result from errors encountered in the software. This implies that the software does not respond in the manner described in the user's manuals (the functional specification). Certain user predicaments may warrant "quick fixes" to the software, at the customer's site, without waiting for a new release. Such quick fixes must be handled with extra care. Corrections of deficiencies normally do not affect the functional specifications or design documentation.

### Refinements

A second category is concerned with requests for refinement of current software. This type of change includes such objectives as performance improvement (e.g., speed), memory utilization (e.g., size requirements), and program structural changes to improve maintainability. Refinement requests generally will not affect the functional scope of the subject software, but will affect the design documentation.

### Enhancement

Software changes may also be instigated by a request for new features, an expansion of existing features and functions, or an accommodation for a new application. These requests generally imply a change in scope, and many have extensive impact on the existing version of the software product. Initiation of the change usually is preceded by a formal plan and change authorization.

### Software Support Overview

Software support is basically a two-step process, from initiation of a system action request until the change is incorporated into a new operational release. The first step requires analysis of the request, determination of the best solution, and authorization of prescribed changes. The second step starts with the software change authorizations and contains all steps necessary to ensure reliable implementation in a future release. These processes are best described in the context of a typical software support organization.

## 9.3 SOFTWARE FUNCTIONAL ORGANIZATION

Figure 9.1 is a generic organizational chart showing the top level of a typical software group. Two functional sections report to the group manager: product development and product support. In addition, a quality control function reports directly to the group manager, which keeps it unencumbered by either of the functional sections. The generic organization shown here is further described in Chapter 10, Section 10.2.

Figure 9.2, the product support section, shows the next level of functional structure. This section is divided into three areas: customer interface, technical operations, and software library.

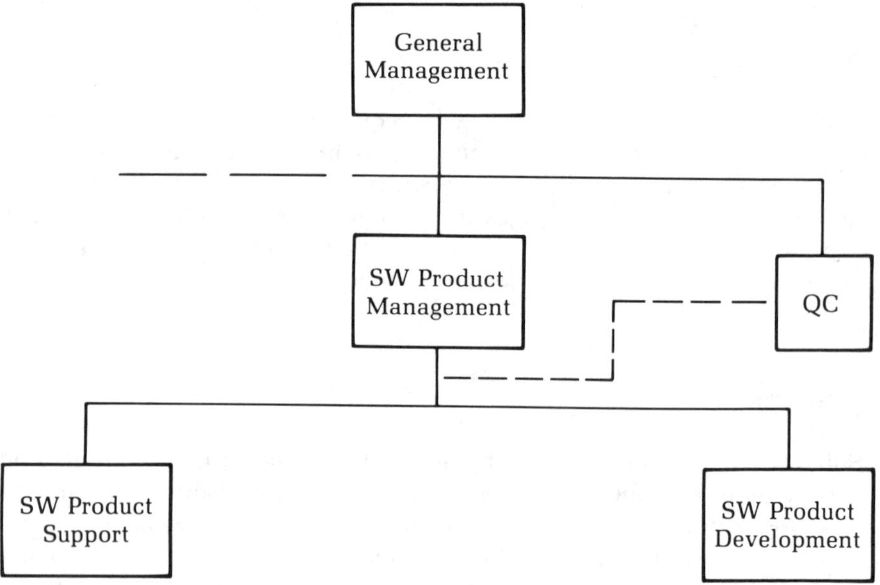


**Figure 9.1.**

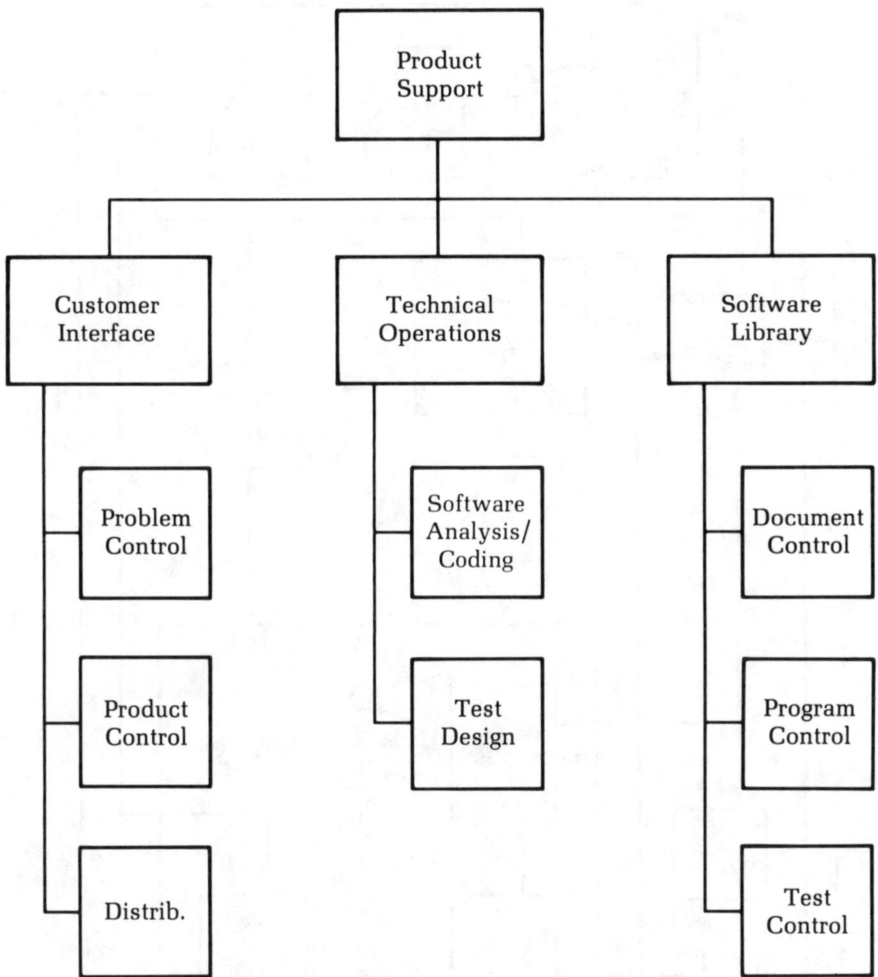


**Figure 9.2.** Product Support Section.

Figure 9.3 shows the interrelationships and utilization of the functional organization elements in support of a software product. The elements in boldface type are elaborated in the following paragraphs.

## Customer Interface Functions

The customer interface team is responsible for three basic support areas, each having in common an interface function with the product customer base.

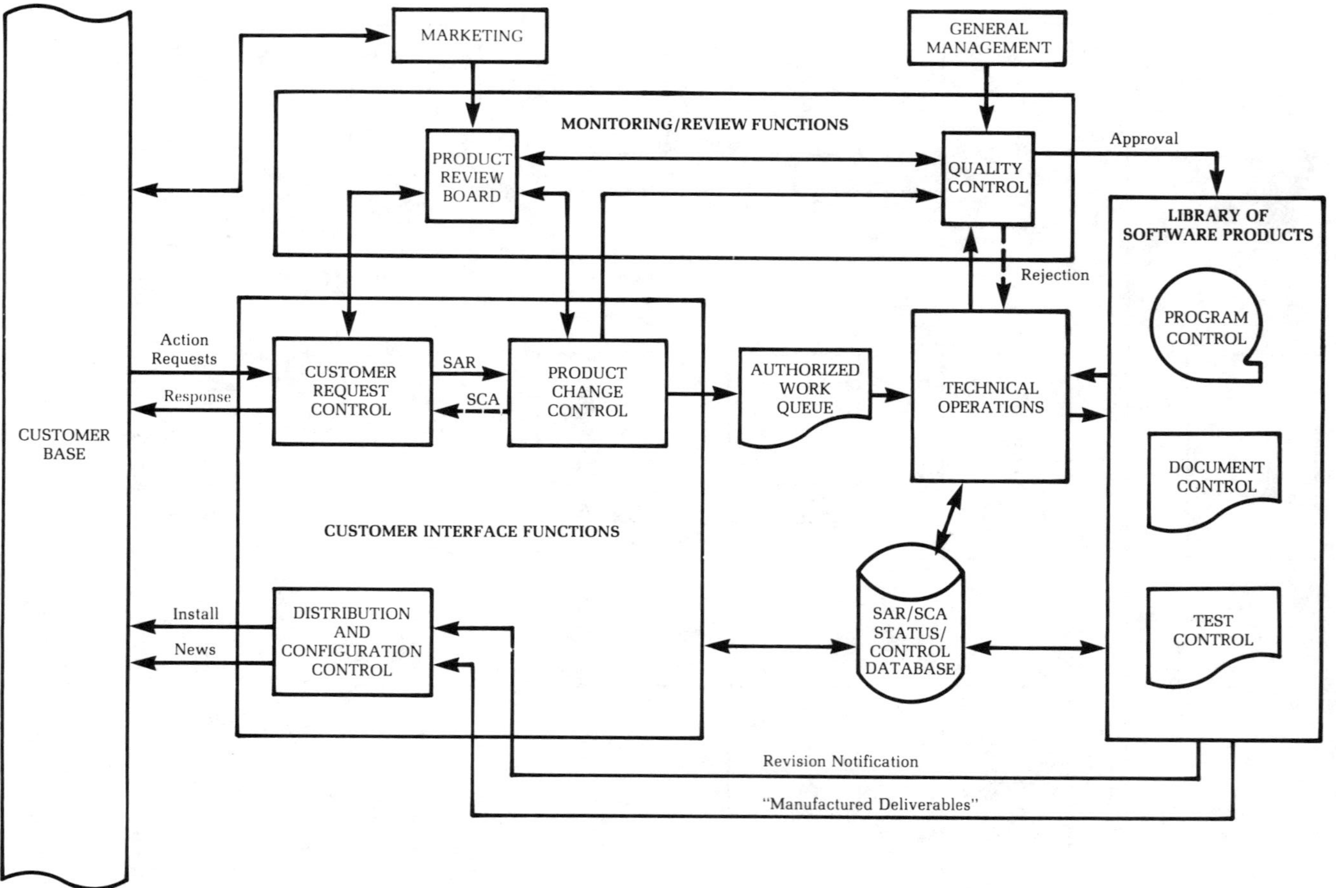


**Figure 9.3.** Organizational Functions For Software Support

*Customer Request Control.* The customer request control function receives or generates system action requests (SAR) from customers and tracks their dispositions. This function analyzes the requests and determines appropriate solutions. It also has the responsibility to respond promptly to the customer regrading the request. A standard SAR form, shown in Figure 9.4, is the primary vehicle for recording and monitoring progress of reported requests.

*Product Change control.* The product change control function authorizes work for all changes to be acted on by technical operations. Product control will also consider implementation priorities for software enhancements or features requested from marketing. A standard software change authorization (SCA) form, shown in Figure 9.5, normally is provided to track program change decisions and status.

Each software change is classified in terms of the type of change and the urgency. Each then is assigned an implementation priority based on descending order of urgency. The change authorizations then are passed to the technical operations function, with the implementation queue being on a first-in, first-out (FIFO) basis according to assigned priorities (that is, all A before start of B; all A on FIFO basis).

*Distribution and configuration control.* This function handles all of the shipment and installation support of software packages to the customers. To fulfill an order, the distribution function requires two basic inputs:

1. A configuration form from the user defining all features and system configuration parameters (i.e., the customer's order)
2. A software package "manufactured" by the software library containing the latest release on specified media and the required supporting documentation

The distribution function prepares a packing list of all deliverables, including a letter of transmittal, and it ensures that newsletters accompany all new releases. This function also maintains a file of all customer installation configurations and revision levels. Such a file (or database) serves two purposes:

1. To provide a convenient status reference for determining which customers should or should not be automatically updated by new releases
2. To provide a reference file when system action requests are received

SAR
SYSTEM ACTION REQUEST

SAR Request Number ______
Suspense Date ______
Request Date ______

System ID ________________________________________
________________________________________

Requester's ID ________________________________________
________________________________________

**Request Type** ☐ Clarification ☐ Functional Change ☐ Error

**Priority** ☐ Urgent ☐ ASAP ☐ Background

**Description of Request** (Attach sheets as necessary)

**Comments** (Attach sheets as necessary)

| SCA Reference Numbers | **Action Scheduled** | | | **Request Closed Out** | | |
|---|---|---|---|---|---|---|
| | Release | Signature | Date | Release | Signature | Date |
| | | | | | | |

**Figure 9.4.**

SCA
SOFTWARE CHANGE AUTHORIZATION

Authorization Number ______

Module ID ______

Software ID ______

Author(s) ______

Suspense Date ______

**Request Type** ☐ Functional ☐ Implementation ☐ Coding

**Priority** ☐ Urgent ☐ ASAP ☐ Background

Authorization Date ______

**Documentation Changes** (Use additional Documentation sheets if needed)

User's Manual ☐ System Overview ☐ Module Descriptions ☐ Database ☐

**Test Requirements** (Describe how module will be tested)

Existing Tests ☐ New Test Required ☐

**Changes to Code** (Refer to program listing) Data ☐ Instructions ☐

| References(s) | **Release Scheduled** | | **Documentation Updated** | | **Changes Tested** | | **Close out Release** | |
|---|---|---|---|---|---|---|---|---|
| | Initials | Number | Date | Initials | Date | Initials | Initials | Number |
| | | | | | | | | |

**Figure 9.5.**

## Technical Operations Function

This function is a resource of experienced analysts and programmers who receive the software change authorizations from the product change control function. The team must be staffed with a permanent cadre of personnel who have in-depth knowledge of the product being supported. Several temporary people also may rotate through this function as they are needed and available. In general, the technical operations function provides a good training ground to introduce new employees to software development.

## Software Library

The software library is responsible for protecting and controlling the software assets of the company. Protection of these assets generally consists of three control functions:

- Documentation control
- Program control
- Test control

*Documentation control.* This function is responsible for setting up and maintaining a control and storage center for all external software documentation. The documents under control by this function include:

- User documents
- Technical support documents
- Standards and procedures
- Technical reports

Documentation control must provide a catalog numbering scheme for all documentation, procedures for controlling the official revision level, and control procedures for distribution of the documents.

*Program control.* This function is responsible for maintaining a control and storage center for all software media. In general, this consists of a set of master files with backup for each standard software product containing:

- Source modules
- Production modules
- Listing files
- JCL files*

Program control maintains an appropriate catalog number scheme for controlling the released revision levels of each software product in the

**JCL is used here in the generic sense of operating system control language. No specific language is implied.*

library. It also establishes and implements a procedure for "manufacturing" deliverable software packages according to a standard configuration request.

*Test Control.* This function is responsible for setting up and maintaining a control and storage center for all test programs and procedures pertaining to the product. This includes all formal test experiments and benchmarks, and the standard regression test library.

## 9.4 OPERATIONS AND PROCEDURES: THE PRODUCT SUPPORT CYCLE

To illustrate the operation of the product support cycle, the following discussion traces the resolution of a typical problem reported by a customer. Figure 9.6 is a general flow diagram of the system action request (SAR) handling process. Each SAR received passes through a five-phase cycle of processing.

| *Processing Phase* | *Responsible Support Function* |
|---|---|
| I. Registration | Problem control |
| II. Evaluation and response | Product control/problem control (with assistance from technical operations) |
| III. Resolution and testing | Technical operations/quality control |
| IV. System integration | Technical operations/library |
| V. Distribution | Distribution |

### Phase I: Registration

When the problem control function receives an SAR, registration should proceed as follows:

1. Assure that *all* the following data is entered on the SAR form:

   - Identification of the customer (or problem source)
   - Date of the initial request
   - Name of the person receiving the request
   - Statement of the request
   - Special consideration relating to the request
   - Preliminary analysis of the request (probable action)

2. Assign a control number to the SAR.
3. Assure that the SAR is accompanied by supporting documentation (e.g., printouts, etc.) when applicable.
4. If data is incomplete or is unclear, contact the customer (or reporter) for further information or clarification.

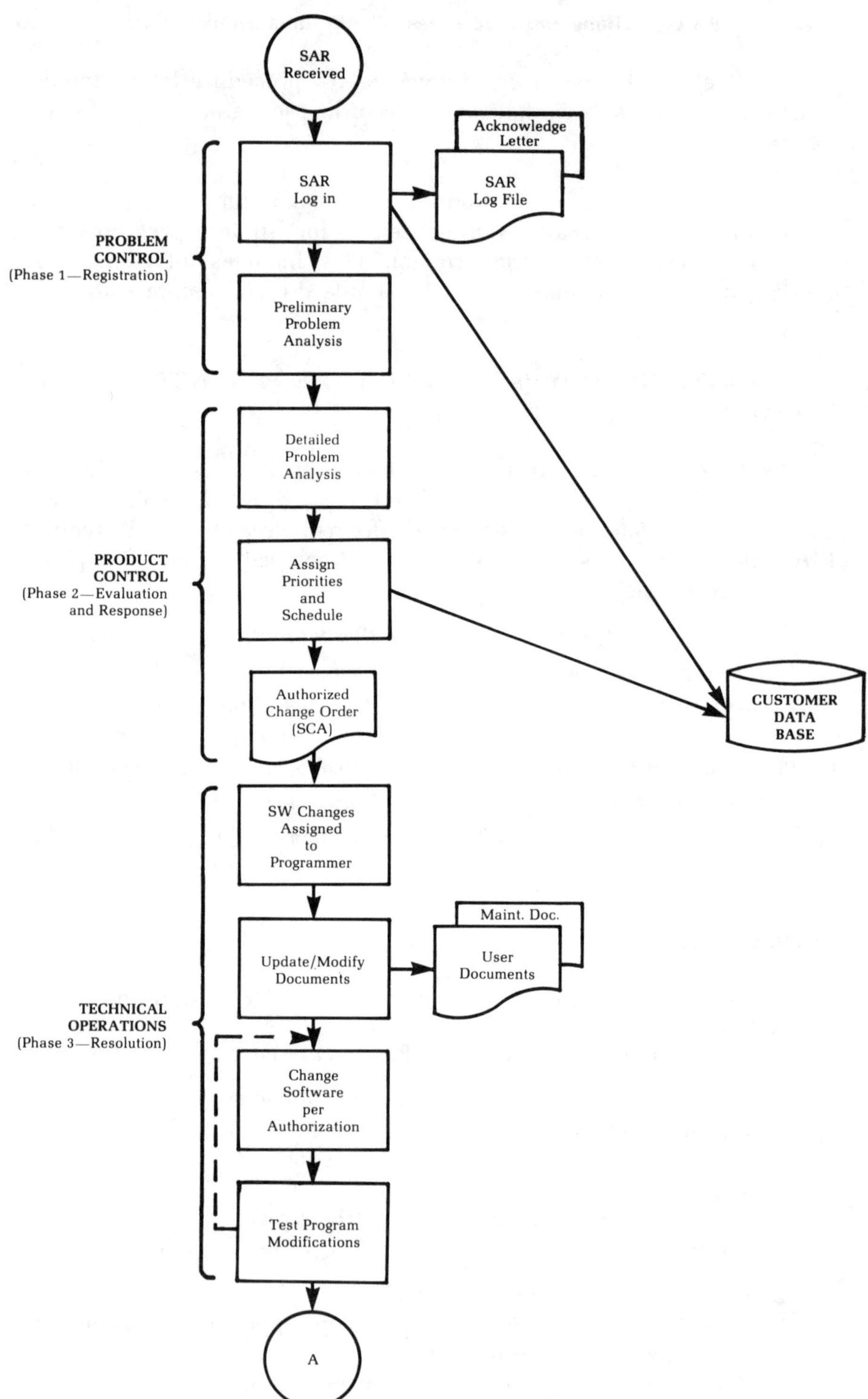


**Figure 9.6.** System Action Request (SAR) Processing.

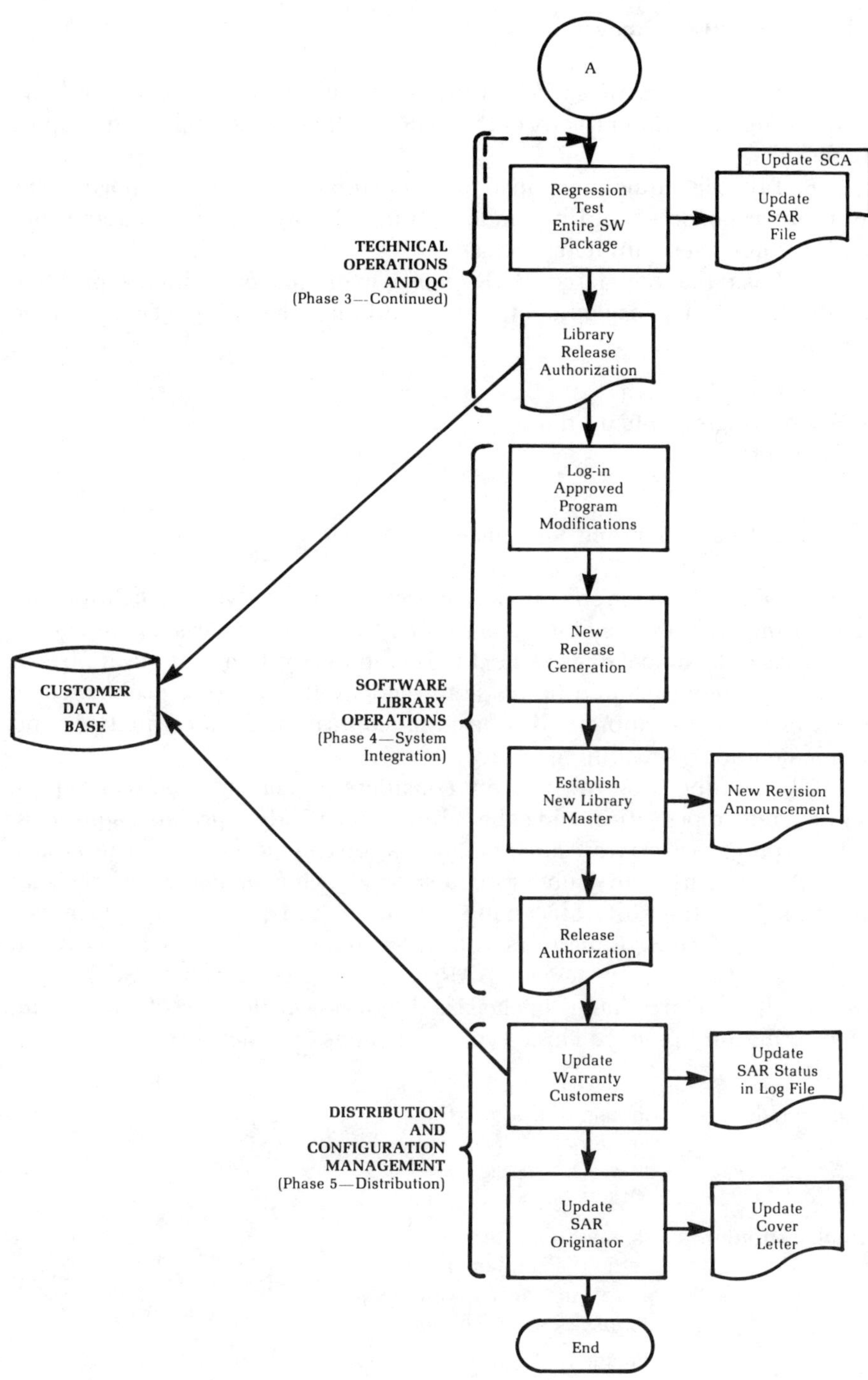

A
Regression
Test
Entire SW
Package
Update SCA
Update
SAR
File
TECHNICAL
OPERATIONS
AND QC
(Phase 3—Continued)
Library
Release
Authorization
Log-in
Approved
Program
Modifications
New
Release
Generation
CUSTOMER
DATA
BASE
SOFTWARE
LIBRARY
OPERATIONS
(Phase 4—System
Integration)
Establish
New Library
Master
New Revision
Announcement
Release
Authorization
Update
Warranty
Customers
Update
SAR Status
in Log File
DISTRIBUTION
AND
CONFIGURATION
MANAGEMENT
(Phase 5—Distribution)
Update
SAR
Originator
Update
Cover
Letter
End

5. Initial the SAR as duly registered and entered into the problem control function. Enter a copy of the SAR into the log file, including support material.

6. Provide a quick response to the customer or problem reporter. The written response should be made within (14) days, acknowledging that activity has been initiated.

7. Pass the registered SAR package on for preliminary problem analysis, priority assignment, and solution scheduling. The package consists of:

- Original SAR form
- Supporting documentation
- SCA forms

## Phase II: Evaluation and Response

In this phase, problem control does a preliminary analysis of the problem, consulting with the technical operations function if necessary, to clarify priorities or technical questions. If the computer system configuration is at hand, an attempt should be made to recreate the reported problem. The SAR form then is submitted to product control for detailed analysis and implementation scheduling.

The Product Control function considers implementation techniques, system cut-in priorities, and scheduling of the pending problem solutions. At this point the software and documentation changes necessary to satisfy the SAR are sufficiently understood so that each change can be precisely described on the software change authorization (SCA) form. Changes imposed by each SAR may generate one or many SCA forms, as shown in Figure 9.7. Conversely, several SARs may reduce to a single SCA.

Each software change is classified in terms of the type of change and the resolution urgency. Three types of changes are defined:

| *Type* | *Definition* | *Affected Documents* |
|---|---|---|
| Functional | Change that alters the functionality of the subject software | User documents<br>Program maintenance documents<br>Listings |
| Implementation | Change that alters the method of implementation, algorithms, speed, storage, etc. (e.g., design changes) | Program maintenance documents<br>Listings |
| Coding | Change that alters the coding of software (no function or design alterations) | Listings |

Problems scheduled for action are passed to the technical operations team for implementation and test; deferred problems are placed on a follow-up

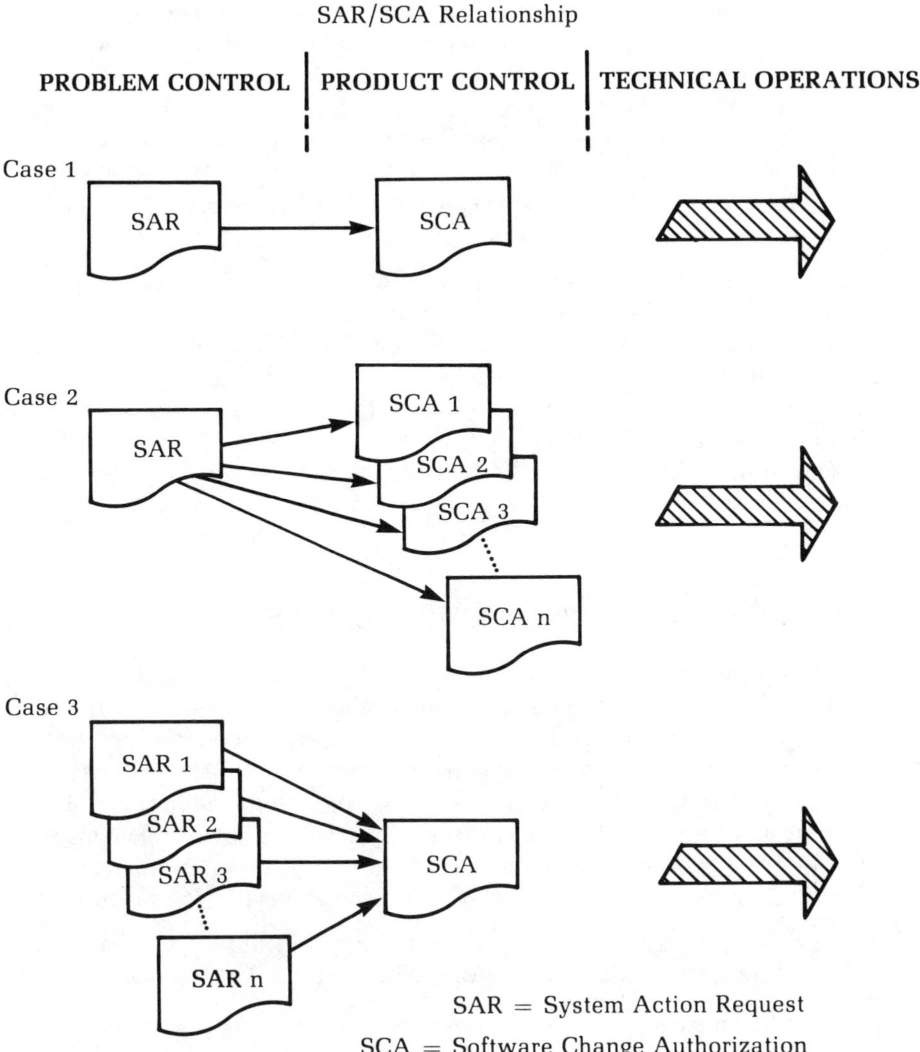


**Figure 9.7.** SAR/SCA Relationship.

list. Each change is assigned an implementation priority based on descending order of urgencies and on a first-in, first-out basis according to assigned priorities. Typically, priorities will be assigned according to the following criteria:

| *Priority* | *Criteria* |
|---|---|
| A | *Urgent:* A critical system malfunction that seriously impedes the customer's use of the product (a problem not previously reported and not part of a planned release). Temporary "patches" between releases also will be considered within this top priority. |

B *As soon as possible:* A system malfunction, not previously reported or part of a planned release, which is not seriously impeding the customer's use of the product.

C *Background:* A problem previously reported and part of a planned release, or a low-grade problem that causes difficulties only under special conditions. This priority is implemented when resources are available.

D *No system problem:* A reported problem that is determined to be operator error or documentation error.

At this point, a second written response is sent to the customer delineating the preliminary analysis of the problem and an estimate of the schedule revision in which the resolution will appear. If on-site software patching for an isolated installation is deemed advisable, the customer will be requested to sign a "waiver of procedures" form by which the customer accepts responsibility for software regression due to the patching operation. The status of all change authorizations is tracked by product control, and periodic status reports are ussued for management.

## Phase III: Change Resolution and Regression Testing

The technical operations function further analyzes the proposed changes in terms of detailed implementation approaches, updates the affected documentation, implements the change, and devises adequate test procedures and routines to assure that the solution does indeed correct the original problem. Changes first are tested with the applicable regression test programs to assure that they have not caused problems elsewhere. Additional test programs, when necessary to verify the solution, then are systematically added to the regression test library. A typical procedure is:

- Run a modified program with the original appropriate regression test.
- If satisfactory, run a modified program with the modified regression test.

When the technical operations function is satisfied that the solution is correct and that the overall system performance has not regressed, the solution package, including the SCA and pertinent updated documentation, is submitted to the quality control function for verification.

*Testing Criteria.* Software testing is defined as a preplanned, structured activity in which prescribed experiments are systematically performed on the software to measure its quality against a specified standard. The standard is a controlled body of test programs called the regression test library.

Regression testing is a mechanism for assuring that the previously established quality for the software is not degraded (or regressed) by changes introduced. The regression test library is a body of test programs derived from the test sets used initially to establish the quality level of the software product. The regression test library must be adaptable to the characteristics of modifications made to the subject software. There are several possible causes for such changes:

- Problem reports from customers
- Enhancements or feature additions required by marketing
- Configuration changes due to changes in existing equipment or to a new system
- Configuration or logical changes

When such changes are approved and implemented, generally it will be necessary to add tests to the regression test base to verify the changes and to assure that they have not degraded the overall system. When quality control (QC) is satisfied that the changes and additional tests have not compromised the integrity of the system, a regression test revision release is made to the test library. The new regression test base then becomes the testing standard for all software delivered to the field. (A new regression test base is established whenever a new release of the software is made. The base will then expand, as needed, by changes made to the release master. This base will live as long as the release lives.)

At any time, the regression test library must be considered the official, reliable benchmark standard that all software packages must meet before shipment to a customer. To assure this, the master regression test library must always be in the possession of the library function. Copies are maintained and must be signed out of the library for a test run and returned to the library immediately afterward. A system verification form, attesting to the successful running of the test, will contain the library number of the regression test used, the date run, and the signature of the tester. The library function must permit no additions or deletions to the master regression test library unless authorized as official.

When additional tests either are added or deleted from the existing base, thereby creating a new reference base, the former base level is retained in the test library for backup purposes. It is recommended that at least three levels of backup be retained. Each time a revision is made to the regression test complement, the library must *require* appropriate documentation updates to accompany the change.

### Phase IV: System Integration

Within the control environment of the software library, a system of present, past, and pending revision masters are maintained. At any time, the current master is the only version of the software product from which deliverable copies can be derived. As each change is accepted by the software library, the librarian systematically integrates the change into the pending new release. Test programs associated with each change, which were part of the technical operations validation process, are also added to the new release master regression test.

*Release Generation.* The product review board oversees the condition of the product at all times. It determines the date of a new release and the software changes to be included in that release. The librarian then implements the release generation procedure, including successful running of the regression test authorized for the new release. The pending master then becomes the official master as release $n + 1$; the former master is saved and submitted to archival storage as backup. A new pending master will begin to be built as additional changes come into the library. In summary, the versions of the software product that can exist at any time are as follows:

| *Revision Level* | *Status* |
|---|---|
| Previous release | Archival storage |
| Current release | Authorized for distribution |
| Pending release | Revision in process |

Following the regression testing of the new master, the librarian issues an official release notice, authorizing the new master for the generation of deliverables and for distribution.

## Phase V: Distribution

The distribution function handles all of the shipment and installation support of software packages to the customers.

*New Customer Deliveries.* The following is a step-by-step description of a typical delivery procedure to a new customer:

1. An order comes to the distribution function with a completed configuration sheet.
2. The order is reviewed for standard or nonstandard handling (e.g., special installation or acceptance requirements, etc.).
3. The configuration is reviewed for completeness.
4. The distribution function requests the software library to prepare the appropriate deliverables.
5. The library assembles the required deliverables, tests the software package, updates the customer file, updates the status file, and prepares a packing list.
6. The distribution function verifies that all deliverables are ready for shipment and authorizes the librarian to ship.

*Customer Updates and Support.* Following the generation of a new release, an updating schedule is established for the warranted customer base. The following is a step-by-step description of the update procedures:

1. Each configuration is reviewed by the distribution function to resolve any potential problem the new release could create.
2. The distribution function prepares a general memo, stating the features of this new release.
3. The distribution function requests the software library to prepare the appropriate deliverables for each authorized update.
4. The library assembles the required deliverables, tests the software, updates the customer file, updates the status file, and prepares a packing list.
5. The distribution function verifies that all deliverables are ready for shipment, and the librarian ships the deliverables, including a cover letter, feature memo, and possibly a newsletter.
6. The distribution function follows up to assure that the update is successfully installed and tested at the customer site.

## Monitoring and Review Functions

The following functions shown in the product support cycle of Figure 9.3 are not part of the normal processing sequence. That is, each provides a monitoring and review of the normal work flow.

*Quality Control.* The basic responsibility of the quality control function is to assure that the established quality level of the released software is maintained or improved when changes of any kind are introduced. Using audits and the regression test standard as a vehicle, QC will certify that the system, as modified by the technical operations team, meets its criteria. To maintain control of quality, the total package—including documentation, source code, object files, listing files, and test sets—must be kept under library control.

*Product Review Board.* The product review board (PRB) functions as an overseer. Its purpose is periodically to review the workflow through the problem control/product control function of the product support cycle and to consider implications to other related functions and/or marketing interests. In essence, the PRB has advice-and-consent responsibility for the workflow through the product support cycle. The board consists of representatives of the development and support groups shown in Figure 9.1, as well as the responsible QC person. It must be chaired by the responsible marketing product manager, with the software product manager serving as deputy. If consensus cannot be reached, the decision must be left to marketing.

## 9.5 PRODUCT MAINTENANCE

This section discusses the methods and procedures for controlled updating and maintenance of a software product and its documentation. To maintain the integrity of the software and documentation, the user and maintenance documents must be reviewed and modified prior to modifications to the software. The approved updated documentation then will be part of the approved change package submitted to the library. A documentation update will always accompany a software release; occasionally, document updates may also occur between releases.

### Document Change Control Procedures

The general steps involved in the documentation library change control are outlined below (refer to Figure 9.8).

1. Technical operations requests duplicate copies of pages of documentation that need changing. The librarian is requested to log the initiation date and the description of the changes to be made, indicating pages to be changed, on the appropriate change record forms.
2. Technical operations makes the required changes to their private copy.
3. Changes are submitted to the appropriate level of management for final approval.
4. SCAs with approvals and supporting documentation are submitted to the librarian for update of the documents.
5. The librarian incorporates the changes into the working copy directly and updates the change record accordingly.
6. The librarian sends the change control packages to a word processing or typing facility to get new originals cut at specified intervals.
7. The librarian incorporates the new pages into the original and working copy files and updates the change record and document control number accordingly.
8. At specified times the librarian releases (temporarily) originals to the distribution function.
9. Distribution coordinates reproduction of updated pages and cover sheet as well as the new documentation set.

### Document Change Record

The document change record provides an instantaneous "snapshot" of where each document stands with respect to changes since the last formal

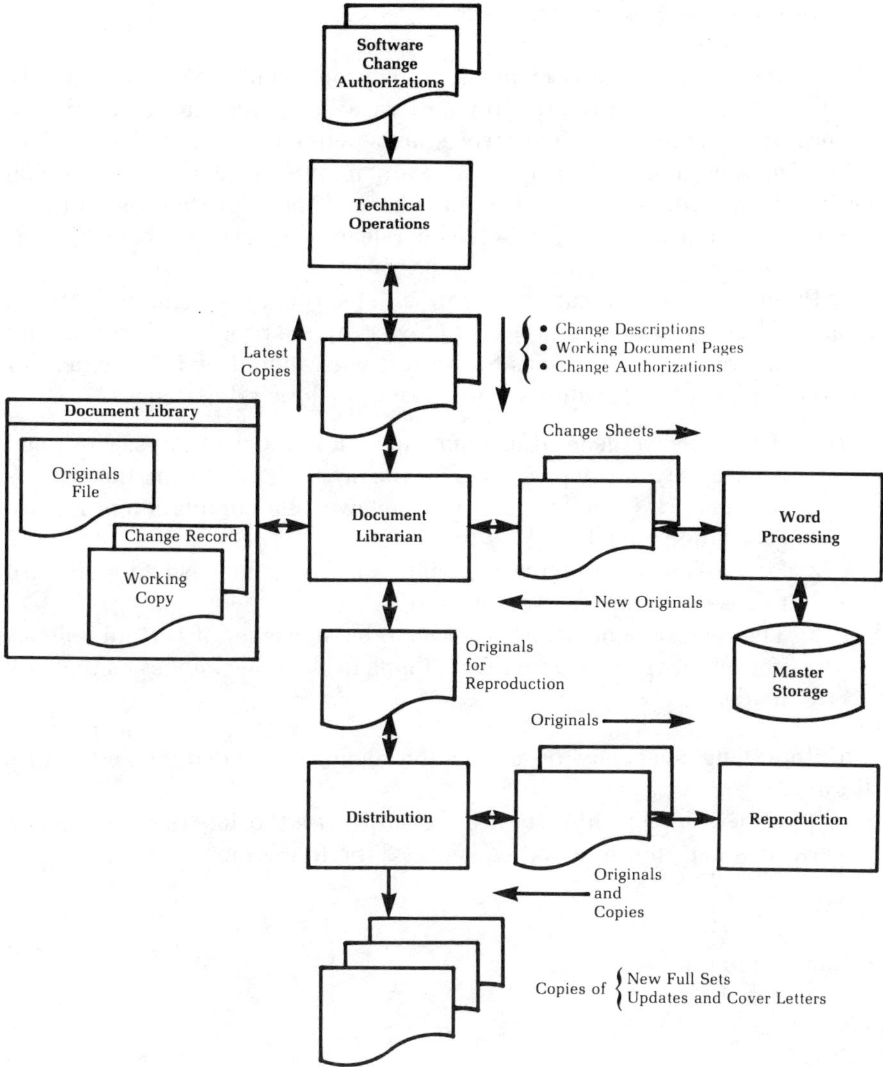


**Figure 9.8.**

release of that document. This record contains a log of changes, from the date of initiation of a new release of the document. It contains the date of initiation of the change, pages to be changed, a brief description of the change, the date the working copy was updated, and the date the originals were updated. When a new release of the document is generated, all open items are transcribed to a new change record to cover the next release.

## Program Change Control Procedures

Procedures for controlling changes to the program library depend highly on the computer hardware and software environment in which the program is maintained. The procedures defined here are designed to minimize the time and cost of program maintenance while achieving sufficient control over the program library. These procedures address control of program changes between releases as well as control over generation of a new release.

Program changes can occur in a "steady-state" fashion between releases. Ideally, procedures to be followed by the program librarian and programmers making changes to the software should be independent of release generation procedures. This provides three advantages:

1. If the release generation time spans a number of days, work can proceed to modify programs for the next release during the generation period. Programmers need not wait for completion of release generation to get back to work.
2. Final determination on inclusion of certain changes can wait until release generation is under way.
3. The release generation period can be shortened if certain policies are set down regarding the methods for testing changes as they are made.

The following overview describes the elements needed to make up a library.

1. *Coded media library:* The existing and prior release backup generally is kept on tape and consists of the following:

*Current Release*

- Source modules
- Object modules
- Load modules
- JCL files
- Test files

*Safekeeping.* Safekeeping, as used here, implies storage of the most recent prior releases, including the current release, for immediate recovery from an unexpected loss (usually due to a disaster). Safekeeping storage would be located at other than the current physical library location, most likely in a vault. The following should be stored:

- Curent release: source modules, object modules, load modules
- Prior Releases: source modules
- Regression test library

*Archives.* Archives, as used herein, implies storage of prior (historic) releases that are still required to support the existing customer base. Considerations are as follows:

- Source may be required to back up special configurations or to ensure that problems have not occurred because of customers' modifying the source.
- Source should not be given to customers.

2. *Current system disk.* This disk (or set of disks) contains the current working version of the product in preparation for the next release. The procedures written here assure that this disk gets backed up on a regular basis—at least weekly, and daily during heavy change periods. Figure 9.9 shows the disk file organization.

*Released Version.* Files containing the released version must be read-only for everyone except the librarian, who will have write privileges. They will contain the following:

| | |
|---|---|
| Source Modules | Only those being changed since last release; will be stored as released (R), however, and will remain unchanged |
| Object modules | All modules for the subject product; will be maintained in the system library and in a private library (possibly on tape) for backup |
| Load modules | As needed, stored in the R files |
| JCL files | As needed, stored in the R files |
| Test files | As needed, stored in the R files |

*Current Development Version.* Files containing the current development version must be read-only for everyone except the librarian. They contain only those modules that have changed since the last release and that have achieved a high degree of confidence via regression testing. They contain the following:

| | |
|---|---|
| Source | Only those modules that have been changed (these correspond to the pending release object modules). |
| Load modules | As needed to test the development version, stored in the D files |
| JCL files | As needed to test the development version, stored in the D files |
| Test files | As needed to test the development version, stored in the D files |

*Private Library Versions.* If a programmer wants to test a change in a given subroutine, then he or she must modify a copy of the latest source and must create a corresponding copy of the object and load module files. If

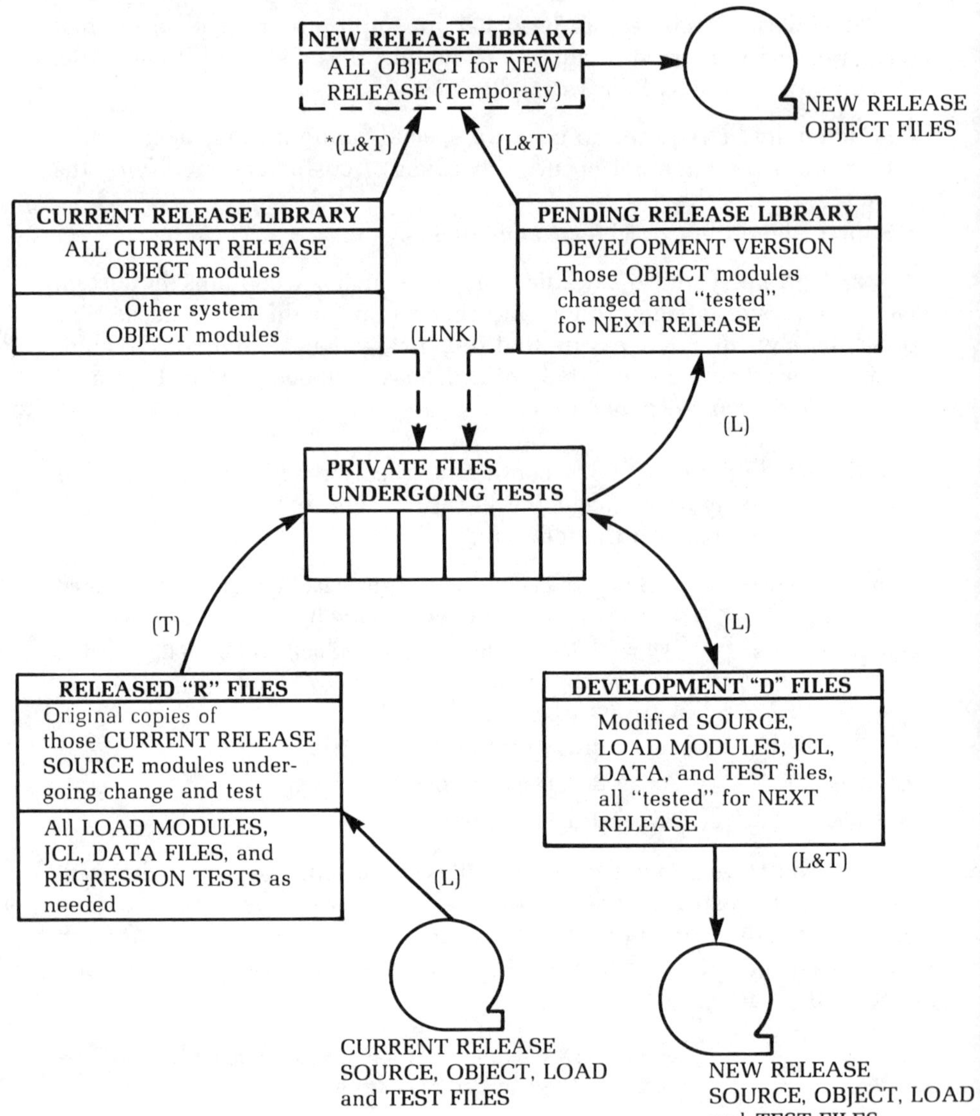


**Figure 9.9.** Disk File Organization.

the development version is to remain unchanged during this process, then such changes must constitute a "private" version. It is the ability to create these private versions that provides isolation between changes introduced by different programmers. Therefore, multiple private libraries generally will exist at any given time. The private library versions contain the following:

| | |
|---|---|
| Source | Only those modules undergoing change by that programmer. Because only one programmer should be working on a given module at a time, only a single copy of changed source modules should reside in the private library area at a given time. When sufficient regression testing is done to warrant confidence that the module is ready for release, then the module is moved to the development (D) library, compiled, and tested again. Upon completion of these tests, unless further work is to be done immediately, the module must be erased from the private library. |
| Object modules | Only those modules needed to link and test the private version |
| Load modules | Only those modules needed to test the private version |
| JCL files | Only those files needed to test the private version |
| Test files | Only those files needed to test the private version |

*Source Listings.* Any routine that has been modified since the last release must be "finally compiled" during release generation. The resulting listing must be put under control of the librarian to be kept in the library of source listings that represent what was just released. Listing of old versions should be moved to the archives or thrown out.

*Change Control Procedures.* The following set of procedures are defined for controlling "steady-state" changes to the program library. Refer to Figure 9.10.

1. Technical operations receives change authorizations previously generated in support of SAR solutions.
2. Technical operations requests the librarian to make the latest versions of source to be changed available on disk.
3. If source to be changed already exists on disk, technical operations is notified. Otherwise, the librarian schedules mounting of current release tape and puts required source into R files on disk.
4. Technical operations copies source to be changed (from R or D files) into the private file and

    - Makes changes to source modules as required
    - Compiles source to private object file

SUPPORTING CHANGE DOCUMENTATION
Software Change Authorization (SCA)
TECH OPS
Request for Source and Test Files to be Changed
Current Release
LIBRARIAN
Source and Tests to be Changed Placed in R Files (or in D)
Source and Test Sets
Appropriate Libraries
TECH OPS, QC
Copy Source and Test Files to Private Library, Modify Compile, Catalog Overlay, and Test
Preliminary Certification and Delete Authorizations
Private Library
LIBRARIAN
Copy Source to D Files, Compile and Move Object to the Private Library, Catalog Overlays, Run Tests, and Delete R Files as Requested
TECH OPS
Delete Private Files No Longer Needed

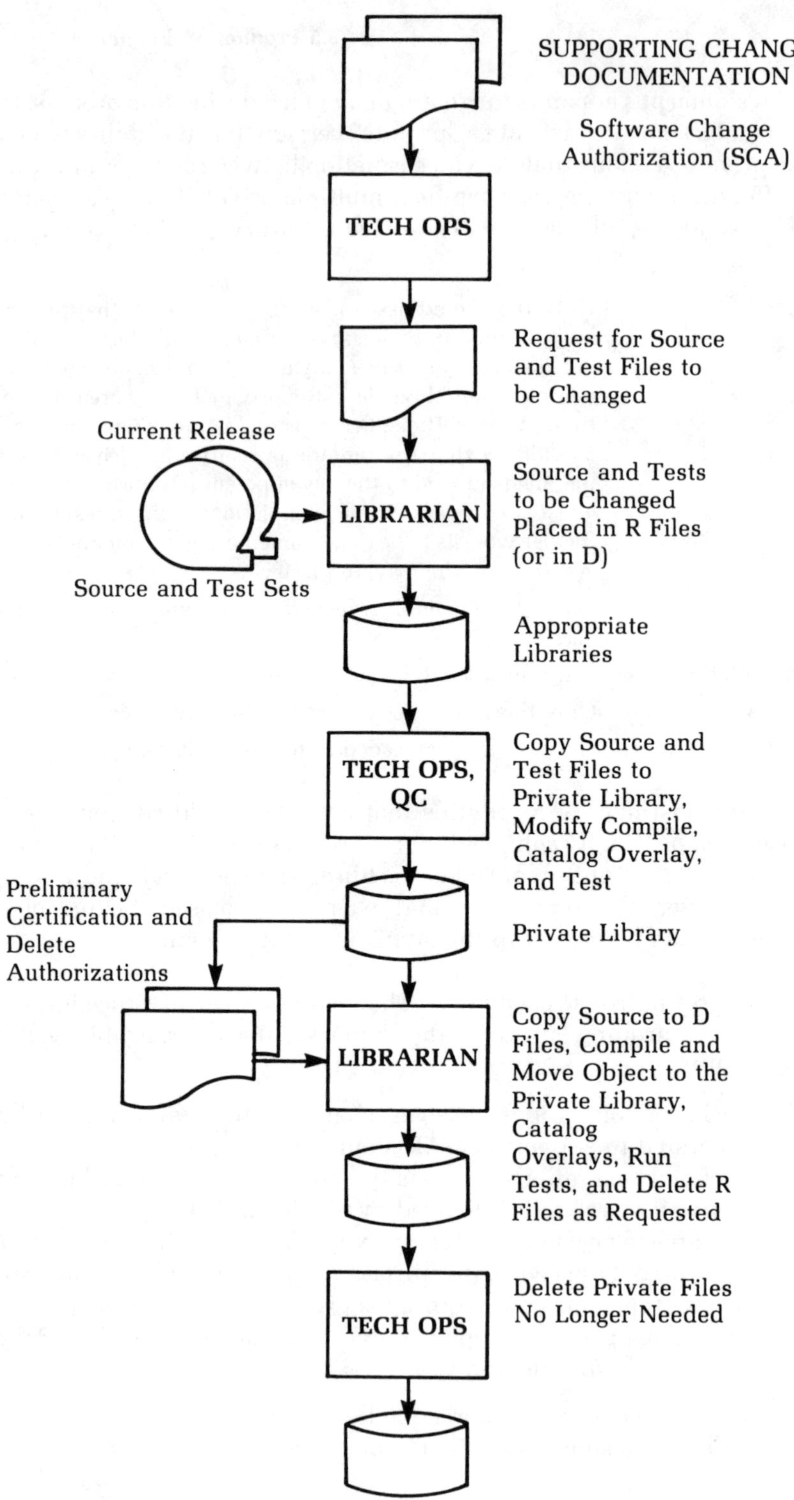

**Figure 9.10.**

- Links the new object modules from private object files to development library and system library, creating a new load module.
- Tests changes using appropriate regression tests and procedures and gets preliminary certification from QC

5. On preliminary certification, the librarian moves the modified source to the D files, compiles and moves the new object to the development library, links appropriate load modules in the development library, and deletes original copy of source from R files.
6. Technical operations deletes private files no longer needed.
7. If it is determined that tests are failing because of a changed module in the development library, the librarian will be requested to delete that module from the pending-release object library so that testing can proceed with the current-release library version.
8. The librarian must obtain authorization from management before deleting modules from any of the following: system library, development version library, R files, or D files.

### Release Generation Procedures

The product review board will define what level of change must be achieved to generate a new release. It will also set a target cut-off date, after which no new changes will be made to the development version of the system. The librarian will be notified of this cut-off date.

The following steps must be performed by technical operations in coordination with the librarian to generate and accept a new release of the software product (Refer to Figure 9.11). Most of the procedures listed can be automated using JCL files for copying, deleting, and compiling routines.

1. Copy the current released version of the object from tape to a private library. Recompile all D file routines and move the resulting object modules into the private library.
2. Link object modules from the private library, yielding all new load modules that contain them.
3. Copy modified JCL and test data into the private library files.
4. Run the release acceptance tests and gain initial sign-off.

### Test Library Change Control

Tests are conducted to ensure that a desired software functional capability exists and provides correct and timely output. When a test is modified, the conclusions that can be drawn regarding functionality generally are modified. The purpose of a regression test is to ensure that when the

Release Generation Menu
Current Release
Object Tape
TECH OPS AND LIBRARIAN
D Files Source
Private Library Temporary (For Release Gen) Current Release Object Modified by Compiled Source from D Files
TECH OPS AND LIB
New SW Release Candidate Core Image
JCL & Release Test Data
Current Release Tape
TECH OPS AND LIB
Run Release Acceptance Tests, Gain Initial Sign Off
Release Acceptance
New Release Tapes
A

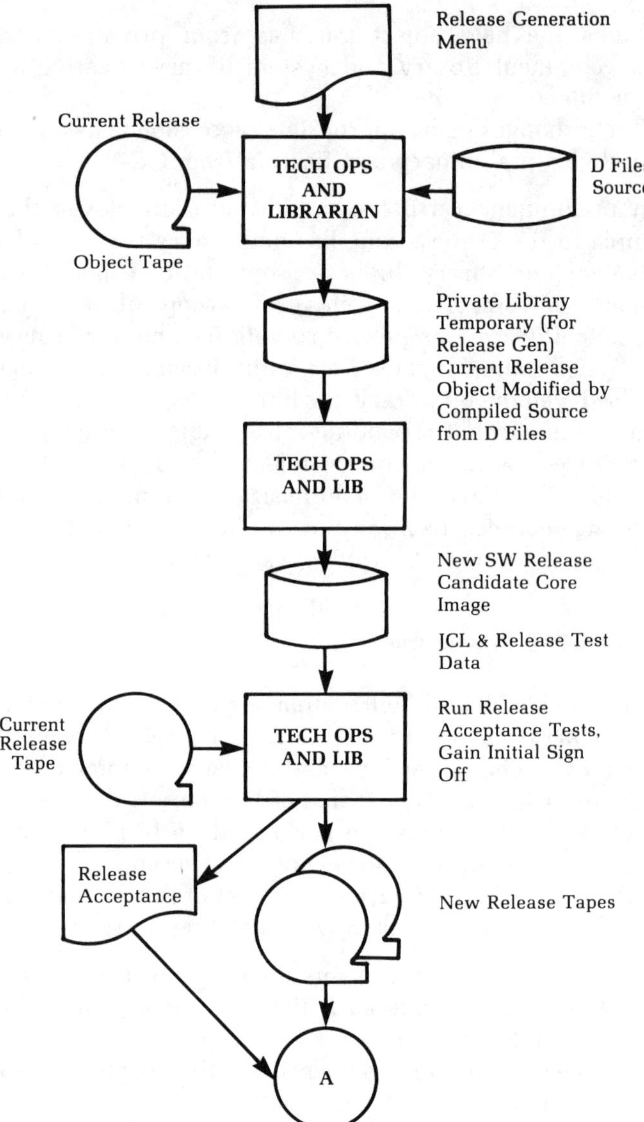

**Figure 9.11.**

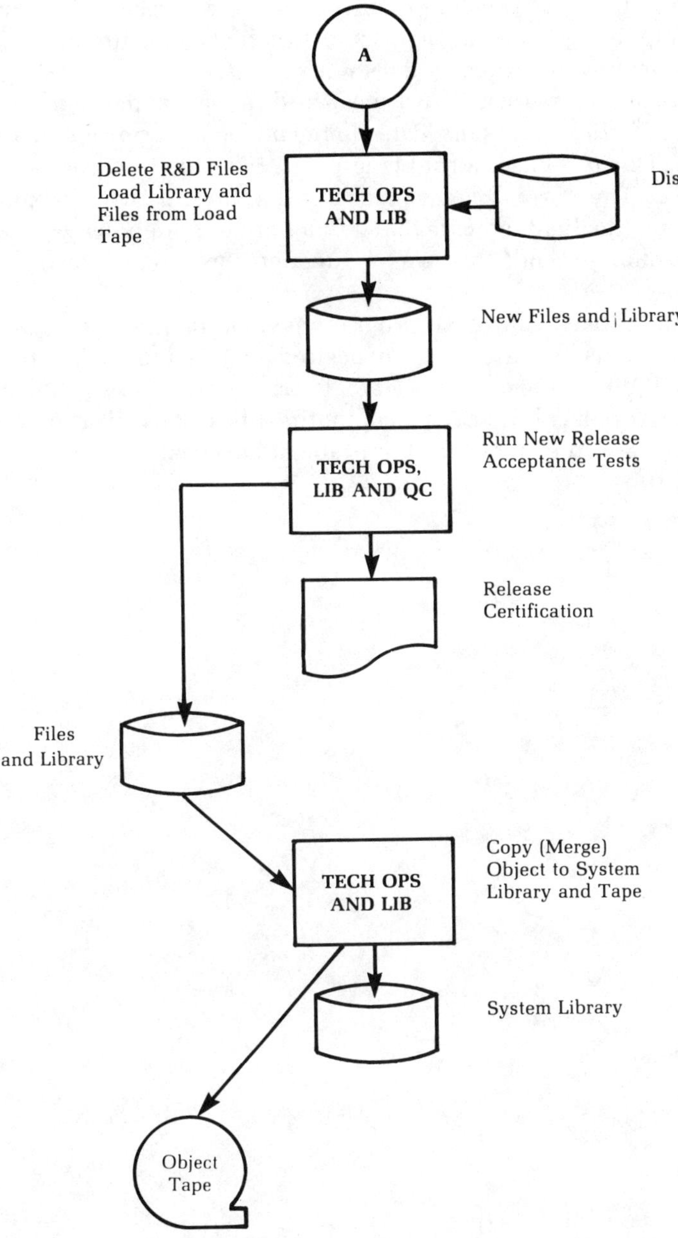
A
Delete R&D Files Load Library and Files from Load Tape
TECH OPS AND LIB
Disk
New Files and Library
TECH OPS, LIB AND QC
Run New Release Acceptance Tests
Release Certification
Files and Library
TECH OPS AND LIB
Copy (Merge) Object to System Library and Tape
System Library
Object Tape

software is modified, system quality has not regressed. The purpose of controlling changes to the regression test library is to ensure that the ability to test system quality does not regress.

By its nature, regression testing affords a reasonable degree of control over test modifications. This is due to the underlying concept of a growing test base. This test base can only regress if, when modified, a desired test is eliminated. The normal consequence is that after a new system release, reports from the field indicate that a function that previously worked is no longer available. And, this was a function for which a test previously existed.

When a particular test program is modified, the change control procedures must ensure that no desired test is reduced, inhibited, or eliminated. When a test is created to determine whether a problem (error) in the software has been corrected, that test first must be run against the current release to ensure that the problem is repeated.

# CHAPTER 10

# The Software Environment

## 10.1 INTRODUCTION

The computerization of America is reaching epidemic proportions. Demand for software to perform ever-expanding computer applications is outgrowing the industry's ability to produce it. This gloomy outlook stems from the fact that writing workable software to meet established requirements historically has proved to be costly and time-consuming. It has consistently resisted the kind of cost-saving breakthroughs that have characterized the hardware side of the computer business. Even though there has been significant progress in software methodologies and disciplines, software development remains substantially a labor-intensive and unpredictable effort. After years of attempts to harness the software problem, creating software is still more of an art than a science.

Much has been written about the creative process of computer programming, and various structured methodologies and procedures for converting algorithms into programs have been devised. This book has presented an important component of the equation, an effective management control methodology. Part of this software development methodology is the environment in which the technical teams and managers must work.

## 10.2 SOFTWARE ORGANIZATION

Figure 10.1 shows a representative software functional organization similar to the matrix-type organization described by Daly (1979). Such an organization can provide a concentrated and controlled environment for building, supporting, and safekeeping a growing base of software assets. The functions of the matrix elements shown in Figure 10.1 are described in the following paragraphs.

### Software Development

The software development function supplies the skill resources required to plan and execute software development projects and software product lifecycles. This includes defining the software problem, detailed planning, time and resource estimation, proposal writing, functional analysis and specification, environment analysis and specification, design, develop-

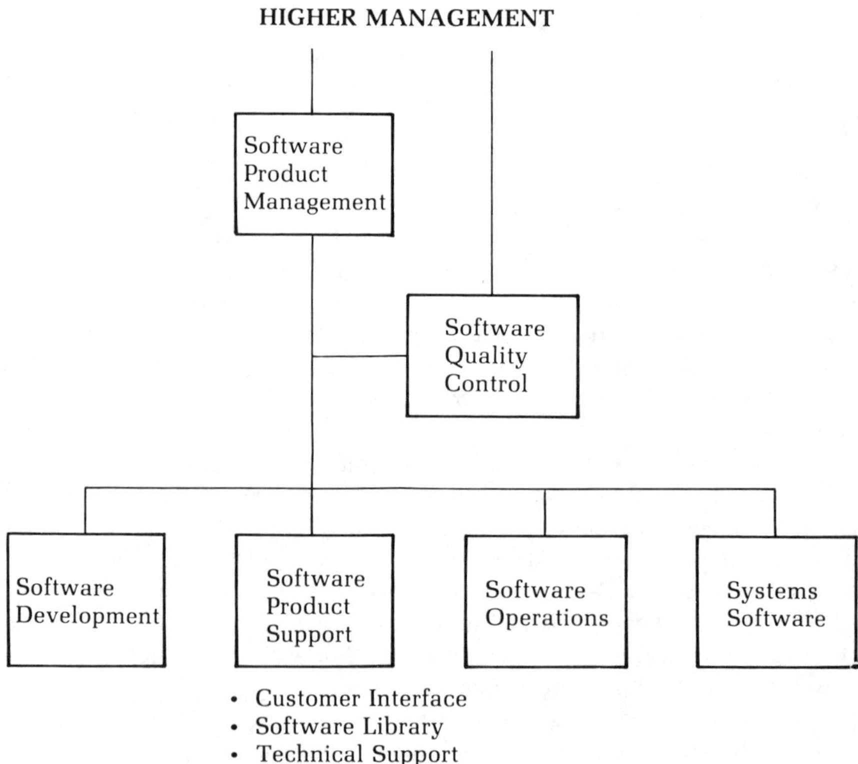


**Figure 10.1.** A Matrix Software Organization.

ment, and prerelease testing. Managers of projects that are primarily software in nature fall into this group. Team leaders responsible for supporting projects managed from outside the software area may also fall within this function. Standards for documentation, programming, testing, and quality control of software that is to be applied to the software development effort may be generated within this function, with exceptions justified on a project or product basis.

### Software Product Support

Two major differences between hardware and software warrant a modified organizational approach to software production and support efforts. First, each time software is "maintained," the design is changed. Software does not "wear out" as hardware does; there are no "replacement parts." Second, one would usually not build into hardware the complex systems built into software. Hardware is too difficult to change. Software is used because it is relatively easy to change. Statistics on successful software products indicate that 60 to 90% of the software maintenance support resources are spent on enhancements to the functional capability. This process can continue for 5 to 15 years for a given product. Personnel turnover is a major consideration, along with protection of the assets (embodied in the documentation, program, and test libraries) as they constantly undergo change.

A breakdown of the software product support function is briefly described in the following paragraphs. A more detailed discussion is given in Chapter 9.

*Customer Interface.* One of the product support activities is a function for receiving customer or internal problem reports, resolving actions to be taken, and soliciting solution recommendations for the reported problems from the technical support functions. Problem reports are translated here into change orders to the software libraries and then are diligently tracked until finally solved. The interface function is also responsible for the distribution of new releases of software products to the existing customer base and the installation of new customers.

Responsibility for customer training on the use of the products may also reside within this functional area. Entry- or junior-level software and clerical skills normally are sufficient for this function, supported by ample knowledge of the application.

*Software Library.* Another important software support activity is a facility protecting the basic software product assets (e.g., the document library, program library, test library, version and release control records, and configuration control). With proper procedures and standards in place, the library can be realized by a high-level clerical function supported by lower level software backup skills when necessary.

*Technical Support.* This function maintains a pool of skill resources to provide technical support across software product lines. It provides the technical expertise needed to interpret difficult problems, recommend changes, implement approved changes and generally to support the previously discussed functions as needed. This function should be a core group of medium- to high-level software technical persons responsible for doing but not controlling. Technical persons newly assigned to the software area may start in this function to gain familiarity with a software product before assignment to new development projects. Organizational flexibility should also exist between this function and the software development function so that skill resources can easily be allocated based on need priorities.

## Software Operations

This function is responsible for the maintenance and operation of the physical computer facilities required for development and support of software products. Planning, aquisition, maintanance, controlling, and scheduling of computer facilities are typical activities of this function. Knowledge of available computer vendor hardware and support software, telecommunication facilities, and peripheral products are important attributes of this function's personnel.

In addition to in-house computer facility management, this function may also supply rental of time-sharing services where they can be shown to be cost effective. Heirarchical library storage facilities and security interactive edit, compile and test, and symbolic debugging facilities provided by this function may cut manpower costs significantly, may speed up development, and may improve overall control of the software development process.

## System Software

This function often serves three purposes. First, it provides the special software expertise when changes and interfaces to the standard operating system (OS) are required for a development project. Second, the selection or creation of OS-related development support tools (e.g., precompilers, librarians, self-test aids) may also require the same special expertise. Third, this function is a convenient consultation center for problems relating to the usage, performance, or service features of the standard software operating systems used by the software development projects. Although people with such specialized skills could be placed within the software development and operations support functional areas, there are personnel attraction and retention considerations that may warrant separate grouping.

### Quality Control

Quality control typically is a review and audit function. The only "doing" type of task normally found in this function involves participation in the modification of standards and procedures. This function is normally attached at the staff level of the software area, but should have a direct reporting channel to higher management to ensure its functional independence.

## 10.3 SOFTWARE TECHNICAL ENVIRONMENTS

The term "software" is an all-encompassing word covering a wide variety of programming products. Development and maintenance effectiveness for may types of software products largely depends on the software development environment provided for the technical staff. An efficient software development system improves productivity by liberating programmers from unnecessary routine work, by automatically coordinating the program development efforts of different persons on the same project, and by providing systematic means for producing high quality software and supporting documentation.

The specific configuration of a software environment must be closely tied to the nature of the software products to be developed in order to be most cost effective and to afford maximum support to the technical staff. One important consideration in establishing an efficient software development environment is an emphasis on in-house support software to support the development and maintenance of the end product applications software.

Figure 10.2 shows the distinction between host and target computing systems. A host computing system is one on which an application software product is developed and is necessarily fully equipped with a wide range of support and utility software. The host is also the system necessary to fix or modify an application's software product. A target system, on the other hand, is the system on which the application's software is to ultimately operate in the end user's environment. In some cases, such as commercial computing centers, schools, scientific research

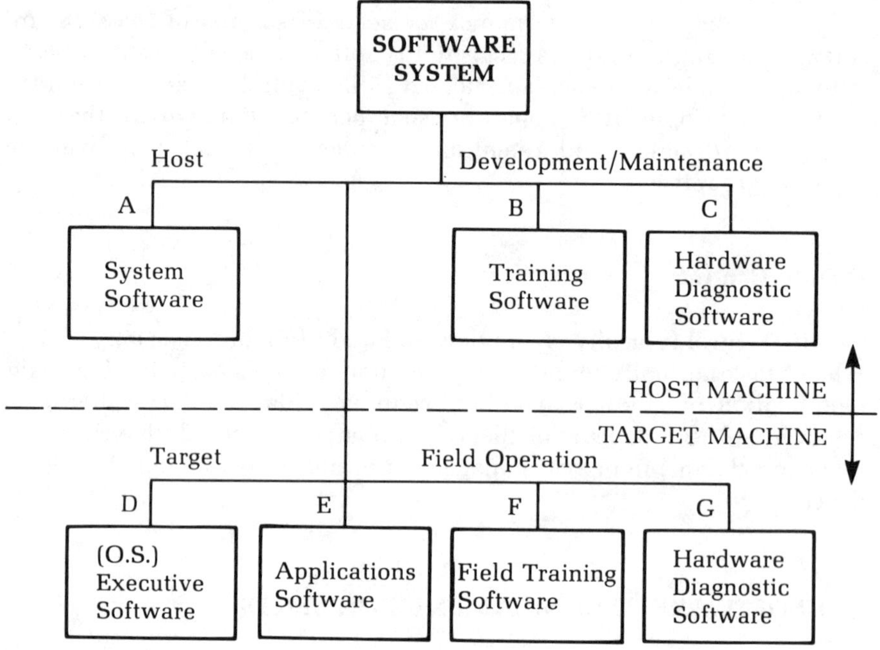


**Figure 10.2.** Host and Target System Relationships.

centers, or any large-scale mainframe installation, the host and the target systems may be the same. In other environments, such as commercial "turnkey" systems (point of sale systems, air line reservation systems, small accounting systems), process control systems, or military field computers, the host and the target systems are often considerably different. For environments in which the end user's target system configuration is compatible with the vendor's host system, a full range of support software can be provided at the end user's site that will permit software updating and maintenance in the field. Such environments also permit the end users to develop their own applications software if so desired. In a turnkey computer environment, it is usually not desirable nor economically feasible to provide facilities within the target system for field development or maintenance. Often the end user of such systems is not knowledgeable in computer usage or programming; the systems are deliberately designed to be used within the context of their intended applications in the same way that an automobile is designed for use by a driver rather than a mechanic. In fact, the support function can fix the software without going near the user's installation.

## 10.4 SOFTWARE DEVELOPMENT TOOLS AND FACILITIES

A host computing center should have all the sophistication with respect to system software capabilities, software development tools, peripheral hardware devices, and languages necessary to make the most efficient, highly productive use of the techincal talent available. A typical modern, medium-scale development environment is shown in Figure 10.3. A centrally located host computing system is provided that can support a community of real-time, interactive terminals located at remote programmer work stations. The host also has the capability to communicate with and down-load programs to a target system.

The host software is capable of simultaneously supporting the interactive terminals in the foreground and a batch job stream in the background. The conversational time-sharing nature of the interactive terminals typically provides each development programmer with a problem-solving work station, complete with system control commands, a library of time-saving development and debugging tools, a word processing facility for program documentation, a selection of program language compilers, and a prompt-driven help system.

A comprehensive host system configuration is only part of the story. A software "craftsman" must have the proper tools to perform efficiently and effectively. The state of the art is currently far beyond the historical software development approach of manual debugging, wholly dependent on the wits and deductive skills of the programmer, with little use of the computer for debugging assistance. Today's "tools" permit extensive use of the host computer to carry out the clerical work necessary to build software properly and to eliminate the inherent guesswork. Some of the generic software "tools" available to today's software practitioners are:

- Structured program design languages (PDL) to clearly map a design. This is the latter-day successor to the classical flow chart
- Structured application-level languages to facilitate structured programming methodologies and to minimize the need for assembly coding
- Interface documenters to generate complete and clear cross-reference documentation at the object module level, thus minimizing interface errors and improving productivity
- Symbolic debuggers to provide interactive debugging facilities at the work station and to accelerate software testing
- Tracing, testing, and optimization tools that can allow management to establish, facilitate, and enforce methodologies and standards for software tracing, testing, and optimization and to provide an audit vehicle for quality assurance
- Word processor to expedite the uniform documentation of source programs and to provide an easy facility for keeping software documentation abreast of software code development

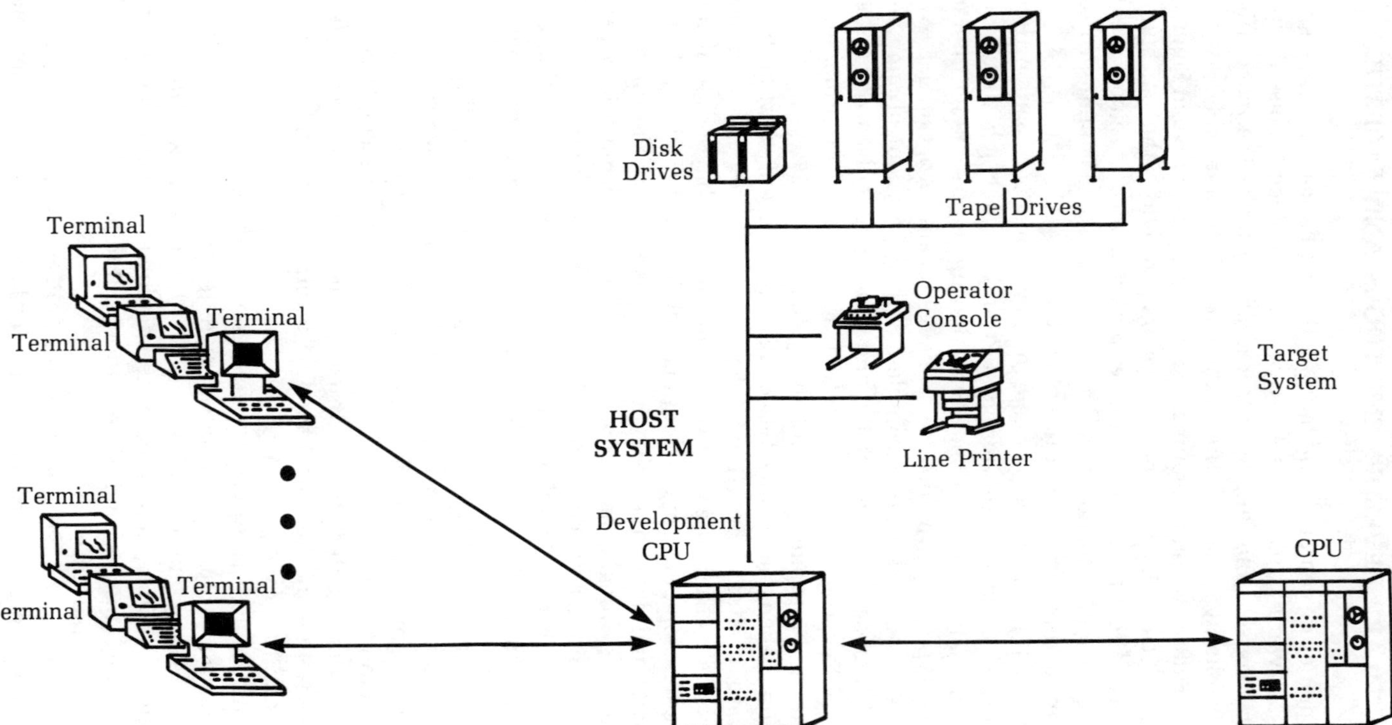


**Figure 10.3.** Typical Development Environment.

- Productivity library to facilitate the use of data structures in structured programming and to allow the use of prefabricated sections of code
- Memory management package to provide the software developer with a selection of dynamic memory managers that minimize the amount of data space required
- Library of preprocessors to facilitate the generation of portable programs between dissimilar machines
- Configuration control facilities to assist in the orderly and consistent management of software revisions and releases. This facility can also support automatic backup and archiving of software modules and programs

Conventional approaches to software development in the past generally have made little use of the computer to assist the programmer in developing quality software products. Today's software tools, on the other hand, make extensive use of the computer to carry out many of the clerical tasks inherent in the development process and, thereby, eliminate much of the guesswork and costly rework that have plagued the software industry in the past.

## REFERENCES

1. Abe, J., et al. "Bankruptcy of Software Projects." IEEE Computer Society Proceedings, Fourth International Conference on Software Engineering, Munich, September 1979.
2. Baker, F. T. "Chief Programmer Team Management of Production Programming," *IBM Systems Journal*, no. 1 (1972).
3. Bloom, S., et al. "Software Quality Control." IEEE Symposium on Computer Software Reliability Record, New York City, 1973.
4. Boehm, B. "Software and Its Impact: A Quantitative Assessment." *Datamation* (May 1973).
5. Brooks, Fedrick P., Jr. *The Mythical Man-Month*. Reading, Mass.: Addison-Wesley, 1975.
6. Cave, W. C., and A. B. Salisbury. "Controlling the Software Lifecycle: The Project Management Task." *IEEE Transactions on Software Engineering* SE-4, no. 4 (July 1978).
7. Daly, E. B. "Organizing for Successful Software Development." *Datamation* (December 1979): 107–9.
8. Dolotta, T. A., and R. C. Haight. "PWB/UNIX: Overview and Synopsis of Facilities." Piscataway, New Jersey: Bell Telephone Laboratories, 1977.
9. Fitzsimmons, A., and T. Love. "A Review and Evaluation of Software Science." *ACM Computing Surveys* 10, no. 1 (March 1978): 3–18.
10. *IBM Virtual Machine Facility/370: Introduction*. Publication no. GC20-1800-8, Poughkeepsie, 1977.
11. Larsen, G. "Software: The Man in the Middle Speaks Back." *Datamation (November 1973)*.
12. Ledgard, Henry F. *Programming Proverbs*. Rochelle Park, N.J.: Hayden Books, 1975.
13. Ledgard, H. G., and W. C. Cave. "COBOL under Control." *CACM* 19 (November 1976): 601–8.
14. Ledgard, H., et. at. "The Natural Language of Interactive Systems." CACM no. 10 (October 1980): 556–63.
15. Mills, H. D. "Mathematical Foundations of Structured Programming." Technical Report FSC 72-6012, IBM Federal Systems Division, 1972.
16. Norden, P. V. "Useful Tools for Project Management." In *Management of Production*, edited by M. K. Starr. Baltimore, Md.: Penguin, 1970.
17. Ogdin, J. "Designing Reliable Software." *Datamation* (July 1972a).
18. Ogdin, J. "Mongolian Hordes versus Superprogrammer." *Info-systems* (December 1972b).
19. Procedures for Management Control of Computer Programming in APOLLO, Bellcomm, Inc., 15 June 1967.
20. Proceedings of the Monterey Symposium on the High Cost of Software, Monterey, Calif., September 1973.
21. Proceedings of the Software Engineering Conference, Garmish, Germany, October 1969a.

22. Proceedings of the Software Engineering Techniques Conference, Rome, Italy, October 1969b.
23. Putnam, L. H. "A Macro-Estimating Methodology for Software Development." In Dig. Papers, Fall COMPCON '76, Thirteenth IEEE Computer Society, International Conference, 138–43, September 1976.
24. Ritchie, D. M., and K. Thompson. "The UNIX Time Sharing System." *Communications of the ACM* 17, no. 7 (July 1974).
25. Sherr, A. L. "De eloping and Testing a Large Programming System." In *Program Test Methods*, edited by W. C. Hetzel. Englewood Cliffs, N.J.: Prentice-Hall, 1972.
26. Snyder, T. R. "Rate Charting." *Datamation* (November 1976): 44–47.
27. *Software Development Guidelines*, Control Data Publication #60418500, July 1973.
28. Spier, M. J. "The Typset-10 Codex Programmaticus." Technical Report, Digital Equipment Corporation, 1974.
29. Stevenson, Henry, ed. *Structured Programming in COBOL*. Proceedings of a Symposium, Los Angeles, 1975 (available from ACM Order Department, Box 12105, Church Street Station, New York, New York).
30. *SYMBUG® Integrated Symbolic Debugging System User Guide*. New York: Computer Associates Incorporated, 1974.
31. Wilbur, M. *Managing Software Reliability: The Paradigmatic Approach*. North Holland, New York: Elsevier, 1981.

# INDEX